LEARNING OUTDOORS

WITH THE MEEK FAMILY

Frances Lincoln Limited
74-77 White Lion Street
London N1 9PF
www.franceslincoln.com

Learning Outdoors with the Meek Family
Copyright © Frances Lincoln Limited 2015
Text ©The Meek Family 2015
Photographs © The Meek Family, except where listed on p176

First Frances Lincoln edition 2015

A catalogue record for this book is available from the British Library.

978-0-7112-3695-0

9 8 7 6 5 4 3 2 1

Printed in China

LEARNING
OUTDOORS

WITH THE MEEK FAMILY

F

FRANCES LINCOLN LIMITED

CONTENTS

INTRODUCTION

Do you enjoy visiting interesting places with your children, and would you like to get the most 'educational value' out of these visits?

Do you support the learning your child does at school with days out in the countryside, or at museums and galleries?

Do you think that what goes on in school is just a small part of a child's broader academic, social and emotional development?

If so, you will find this book a helpful resource because it

- Provides a bank of ideas for making weekend visits to places of historical and cultural interest, entertainment venues and a variety of outdoor environments that are educationally beneficial as well as fun and engaging.
- Encourages children to appreciate and understand the natural and man-made world through the development of enquiry skills and the capacity to assimilate, interpret and evaluate what they encounter.
- Promotes family time in the outdoors, which is beneficial in many ways for both adults and children.

THE RATIONALE BEHIND INFORMAL OUTDOOR LEARNING

It is an outdated notion that education must take place behind a desk in a classroom, with a teacher at the front, disseminating knowledge and wisdom. In a time when technological progress has given us instant access to information, literally at our fingertips, and the ability to travel easily, quickly and reliably to a greater range of areas and places, the outdated Victorian classroom approach is no longer the ideal model for teaching or learning. Taking the child out of the 'bricks and mortar' school to find rich environments can lead to more purposeful and effective learning experiences – learning that is pervasive and ongoing, not bound by walls or compartmentalised by subject areas. Information learning is also more experiential or participatory and therefore results in multi-sensory engagement and deeper learning.

Informal learning that takes place beyond the classroom develops capabilities that are not easily addressed through a class-based approach centred around a 'deliver and receive' model, where the commodity in question is knowledge. Incidentally, this 'industrial approach' is adopted as the favoured system because it lends itself to a 'test, grade and measure' approach, rather than being the 'best' method. This model can sometimes occur at the expense of the development of other, more valuable capabilities such as collaboration; encouraging independence and initiative; higher order skills such as evaluation and interpretation; as well as problem-finding and problem-solving, which are, by their very nature, harder to teach and, more importantly, harder to measure.

Where learning takes place outside of the classroom, outdoors, there is a growing recognition that it has significant value. The time young people spend outdoors is significantly less than that of their parents' generation. The reasons for this include an increasingly risk-averse society, in which children are being wrapped up in cotton wool and kept indoors, where it is warm, dry and safe... and where the games console, TV and home computer occupy them. The upshot is that children are becoming increasingly reliant on technology, yet more disconnected with nature... and, in a lot of cases, increasingly unhappy. Some of the reported benefits of being outdoors include:

- increased physical health
- enhanced mental health
- enhanced sensory and aesthetic awareness.

OUR OWN ADVENTURE

As parents and teachers, we think the role of informal learning, indoors and out, is undervalued. We believe young children need to be given opportunities to spend time outdoors; visiting places, meeting people and learning from them; experiencing, participating in and constructing knowledge, not just acquiring it.

We feel so strongly about this that we decided to make a drastic lifestyle change. We sold our house, quit our jobs and took Amy and Ella out of school to embark on a year-long EdVenture around the UK, living and learning in a caravan, in the hope that it would provide a wealth of stimulating opportunities for our children to be educated 'on location' and through meeting and speaking to people. We hoped that it would provide multi-sensory learning, both supporting and challenging their preferred learning styles, and be rich in experiences. We wanted Amy and Ella to learn about the plight of King Harold in 1066 where it actually took place, to see salmon returning to spawn in Scotland, to learn about coastal erosion on the Norfolk coast – and a whole lot more as well – in the first person, not through an over-reliance on books and videos. Living in a caravan freed us from the shackles of a fixed abode, so we had a mobile base that could be towed in any direction that our interests and passions pulled us.

Our EdVenture has been an exciting and fulfilling experience that has seen us all working and learning together, alongside one another, and having lots of fun. We've been able to tailor our 'caravan curriculum' to make it bespoke for Amy and Ella's interests, resulting in high levels of engagement and a degree of ownership that only comes from self-directed learning. An important by-product from an approach that encourages Amy and Ella to interact with staff at museums, galleries or exhibitions, or local people and experts that we meet when out and about, is a growth in self-confidence and an ability to communicate effectively with different people in different contexts.

It hasn't always been a smooth ride. We have encountered difficulties and setbacks, and we have made mistakes along the way. But are we glad we took the decision? You bet. And would we do it again? Of course. Why not? Life is too short not to, right?

CONTENT & ORGANISATION

The book is organised into 51 mostly outdoor places to visit, explore and learn about. The list is certainly not exhaustive, but it gives an idea of the kinds of places you might want to take the children to for inspiring and enjoyable rich family learning experiences in the outdoors.

Each activity is spread over two or four pages and is structured to make it easy for busy families to dip into. The consistent sections are:

BEFORE YOU GO...

This section focuses on how to prepare for a trip. Before any visit, it prompts a planning activity like looking at maps, carrying out research and the need to think about any specific questions or areas a child wants to find out about.

WHILE YOU ARE THERE...

The activities in this section focus on some of the different ways to learn, such as talking, listening, reading, physical and sensory. The activity suggestions are specific to the type of location and should be used to support your child's preferred learning styles, as well as to challenge them to learn in new ways. Experiential and multi-sensory learning are valid and extremely important, so try a range of activities with your child if you can; don't judge the quality or depth of learning by conventional methods alone, like reading, then regurgitating information.

WHEN YOU GET BACK...

After a visit there are different ways to direct your child's interest. This section provides suggestions for further investigations and generally offers activities that involve:

- making
- writing
- drawing
- presenting
- playing
- doing
- testing

There are also sections designed to stimulate enquiry, to help develop children's self-confidence and self-esteem and, on the longer activities, an odd-one-out challenge.

WHY THE BOOK HAS BEEN WRITTEN

We hope that this book encourages and enables parents and carers to have the confidence and belief to see themselves as important facilitators of their children's learning; as key agents in the educational and broader development of their offspring. Parents and carers know their children better than anyone else – what makes them tick, what grabs their attention and sustains their interest – and as any teacher will tell you, interest and engagement are vital factors for motivated learners. You may not have all the ideas, but that is where this book will help you.

We hope many families enjoy some or all of the 52 EdVentures in this book as much as we have. If you do one every weekend, you'll have a year full of fun and learning!

Now it's over to you. Which one will you choose first?

THINGS TO DO ON A JOURNEY

GAMES TO PLAY ON JOURNEYS TO AND FROM LOCATIONS

Games are the perfect way in which to while away the hours travelling to and from your chosen destination; not only are they fun, they can also stimulate and consolidate learning, as well as keep minds active when the bodies aren't. Value this family time and enjoy the shared period of learning about, with and from your family.

The games listed below attempt to practise key skills such as questioning, listening, memory and problem-solving as well as traditional literacy and maths skills. Many of the games focus on speaking and listening. Research has shown that talking – repeating or explaining – commits facts to memory better than simple listening or reading. Games are a fun way of learning; the kids might not even realise they're doing it! Adapt the games to suit the age and ability of the children playing.

TWO TRUTHS AND A LIE

One person in the family shares three statements or facts about the location that you are visiting. Two of the statements should be true and one should be made up. The 'lie' should ideally sound plausible so that it is not immediately obvious to the other players.

Everyone else who is playing needs to guess which is the lie. If they guess correctly, they win a point, but if they guess incorrectly, the person who made the statements gets the point.

20 QUESTIONS

This is a classic game that focuses on asking questions but, more importantly, listening to others. One player chooses a person, place or thing that is linked to the location that you are visiting, then everyone else has to ask that player questions in order to identify what it is. The object of the game is to guess what it is in less than 20 questions.

THUNKS

Thunks are unusual questions or statements that make you think. They have no right answer and are a great way to make you think differently and prompt discussions, e.g. can you stand in the same river twice?

NUMBER PLATE GAME

Look at the three letters displayed on passing car number plates. Be creative and try to think of a short three-word phrase using the letters, e.g. CRS Can Raspberries Sing?

MAPS

Give the children access to a map or road atlas. Encourage them to trace the journey that is being taken. Take turns to choose a town, village or feature on the map. The others have to guess what it is by asking questions.

CATEGORIES

Prepare a list of categories (these could link to the location that you are going to visit). Each player needs a copy of the categories in front of them. Choose a random letter; this could be selected using a whilygig app on a phone, to make it fair. Once you've got a letter, everyone has a specific amount of time to think of items on the list beginning with that letter.

At the end of the time, everyone reads out their words. If they have an item on their list that no one else has thought of, they get a point.

BLANKETY BLANK

This was a British comedy game show that appeared on television during the late 1900s – some parents/carers/grandparents might be old enough to remember it!

The idea behind the game is that a contestant is given a statement containing a blank (these should be prepared before the journey and ideally link to the location that you are visiting/have visited). The statement is read out to all the players. Everyone writes down what they think should be in the blank.

When playing this with younger children, the aim of the game is to get the correct answer, which can be written on card. Whereas, if playing this with older or more able children, the answers can be more open-ended, in the style of the original game. After a short period of time, the 'contestant' then says their answer. If it is the same as anyone else's they get a point, as well as the person who wrote down the answer. Take turns being the 'contestant'.

DON'T ANSWER THE QUESTION

This is something politicians are very good at! Try listening to some of the answers they give when interviewed on the TV or radio then have a go yourself; it's more difficult than you think.

MAKE A SENTENCE

Set a time limit in which to collect a bank of words (individually or as a group). Words may be objects (nouns) seen out of the window or describing words (adjectives) that could be used to describe them, e.g. an 'old' car. Write down any words that are said. After the set time limit, everyone tries to make up sentences using the words from the list.

ONE-WORD STORY

ABC

Create a story together by taking it in turns to add one word at a time. Each person that plays needs to listen to what is said before them, adding their own contribution to ensure that the story makes sense.

JUST A MINUTE

Just a Minute is a popular BBC Radio 4 game show in which contestants have to talk about a subject for one minute without hesitation, deviation or repetition. A variation of this can be played on a journey and is a fun way to consolidate learning. Give the child(ren) a topic linked to the location that you are visiting/have visited and allow them a minute in which to prepare some notes. This allows them some thinking time, rather than being put on the spot and panicking. Then, using their notes, they must talk about the subject without hesitation, deviation or repetition – how rigidly you stick to these rules depends on your family unit. Award points for successfully completing the challenge.

TREASURE HUNT

This calls for some preparation, but get the children involved. Create a list of things that you are going to look for on the journey. Make the items on the list age-appropriate and appealing to the children.

BUILDINGS
TO SEE

LEARNING AROUND
A WATERMILL/WINDMILL

A watermill is similar to a water or wind turbine in that it converts a flow of water into electrical power. Unlike water and wind turbines though, the power it generates is often used at source rather than being converted into electricity. In previous generations, watermills powered workshops, bread mills and even factories, so were very important.

Windmills get their power from natural resources on site, too. In earlier times the power was used for milling grain or for agricultural and industrial uses.

BEFORE YOU GO...

Your children will probably find it hard to imagine life without the internet or touch-screen technology, never mind electricity. But it wasn't so long ago that electricity became widely available and affordable for the masses – in fact, there are still huge areas of the developed world that still do not have access to a permanent supply of electricity.

Before electricity was available in the Western world, other forms of mechanical power were invented and harnessed. Before you visit a mill, dip back in time to find out about the Industrial Revolution and when it was that wind and water began to transform manufacturing processes. Think about how and why this was important for streamlining and increasing efficiency and capacity for industry and the products associated with watermills and windmills.

Where graining mills are concerned (mills that grind grains into flour for the bread-making industries), there is a need for a set of grinding stones of suitable properties (open-textured and tough). Areas rich in suitable millstone became suppliers for mills, and an important source of income for their local areas. This in itself is an interesting angle to explore.

If you are can, visit a watermill and a windmill so you can compare the two. This will enhance and consolidate your children's understanding of these two once-major power sources. Children like to spot similarities and differences in things, so encourage them to do so here.

Another way to grab children's attention is for them to learn about the roles that young people had in factories and mills during early industrial times. Exploring a mill using a focus like this helps retain interest and empathy, both important aspects of meaningful learning.

ENCOURAGING LINES OF ENQUIRY
- Focus on function – what did the mill produce and what were the by-products?
- What was the role of mills in their heyday versus the mill today?
- Focus on the mechanical elements of mills.
- Location, location, location – why is the mill positioned where it is?

TIPS

- Try to visit on a demonstration day.
- Check opening times before you go. The mill might be open all year round but may only have certain days when it is working or has organised tours.
- Watermills have deep dangerous millponds, so supervise your children at all times.

WHILE YOU ARE THERE...

Go with the flow by following the mechanical sequence of a mill. At a watermill, start at the river that flows into the mill; at a windmill, start at the top, where the wind source enters the building.

Look around. The mill itself is only part of the visit so hunt out buildings and artefacts that help to give you a full picture of what it was like during working times.

Make the experience an interactive one by letting the children get their hands on any tools of the trade that may be available for them to touch or handle.

ENCOURAGING DIFFERENT WAYS TO LEARN

PRETEND to be a Health and Safety inspector during the milling period by looking carefully at any aspect of the mill, or the milling process, that might have risk associated with it. You could even take a clipboard and note down, in a very official way, anything you see.

EMPATHISE by finding out what life was like for children working in the mill at the time and compare it to your daily routines and chores.

USE YOUR SENSES A busy working mill would have lots of smells and noises. Close your eyes and try to sense the mill as it used to be by imagining the activities that would have taken place. Using your nose like this will make the pictures in your head much clearer.

WATCH a demonstration of the milling process and, if possible, have a hands-on go yourself.

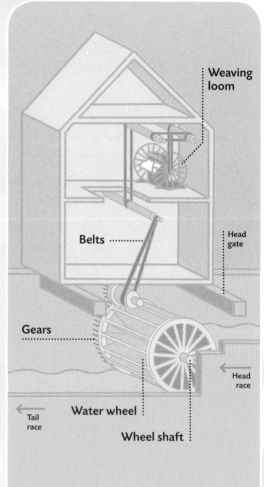

Weaving loom

Belts

Head gate

Gears

Head race

Tail race

Water wheel

Wheel shaft

HOW A WATER MILL WORKS

ODD ONE OUT – FIND THE FAKE FACT!

- The windmills in the Netherlands were used to drain water from the land to enable crops to be grown.
- ✗ The windmill was invented in the UK around 8AD.
- A waterwheel is a type of turbine.
- British gritstone was used for millstones.

BE BOLD

If a volunteer is needed during one of the demonstrations, put your hands up straightaway and offer your assistance; being involved in the demonstration is much more fun than just watching it. Go on, be brave!

WHEN YOU GET BACK...

A trip to a mill can be a great stepping-off point for further work on the mechanics behind a mill. This could be as simple as messing about with cogs, pulleys and friction bands (elastic bands), or something more organised such as trying to make a simple windmill. Construction sets provide a good way of learning about mechanics and physics in a playful way.

SUGGESTIONS

- **FIND** two rough stones and try to grind something between them. Which materials can your stones grind down?
- Try to **COMPLETE** the milling process from where your visit to the mill left off, e.g. buy some of the mill's flour if available and make bread with it. Further research or science work might be required, but that's all part of the learning experience.
- **MAKE** a belt and pulley system using some cotton reels and elastic bands. You may need to search on Google to find out what to do.

LEARNING AROUND
A MUSEUM

A museum is a building that contains collections of items that are of interest for everyone to see. In fact, a museum could be as simple as a single room or a garage full of objects.

Whenever you are visiting a new location, visit the local museum and use it to learn more about the area; these small museums sometimes offer a better experience than larger ones.

BEFORE YOU GO...

Museums can sometimes seem like large, daunting places, particularly the long-established ones in capital cities. If the museum you choose to visit is large in scale, try to focus your time and efforts on a particular section that is in line with your children's passions. Don't try to take in the whole museum – no matter how much it costs to get in. If you do, you run the risk of overload and putting the kids off museums for life! Most museums usually have a hand-stamp system that allows you to take a break outside and have a run around in the fresh air, before re-entering for a second, shorter stint.

Whatever the size of museum you are visiting, another thing to consider before you head out is the purpose of your visit. It may be you are going to a museum to support your child's schoolwork; or with the intention of sparking their curiosity in something specific; or to learn about the locality you are holidaying in. It may be that you are going along just to browse and be surprised. Whatever the reason, make sure you have a specific purpose for your visit; it will make your day much more productive.

ENCOURAGING LINES OF ENQUIRY
- What time-period does the museum cover?
- What is the earliest/newest item in the museum?
- What does the museum tell you about human intelligence and ingenuity?

WHILE YOU ARE THERE...

How much your child gets out of the museum will depend to some extent on their age and interests, but think creatively about ways to engage them with the museum content rather than simply dragging them around aimlessly. That way you will sustain their interest levels.

ENCOURAGING DIFFERENT WAYS TO LEARN

CHALLENGE children to go into a museum area of their own choice for 30 minutes and to find out, and retain, as much as they can. After 30 minutes, they have to take an adult into that area and give them a guided tour. Offer to pay them a pound (dollar) or two if they do a good job – this is sure to grab their attention.

ACT out scenes from the artefacts on display, or the historical period they represent. Some museums have dressing-up clothes for the kids to try on, which enhances the experience.

LISTEN to the museum's audio tour. There may be a charge for this, but it is usually worth the fee and will engage and empower your child as they peruse the museum at their own pace...

Encourage your child to **PLAY DETECTIVE** by finding the three most valuable artefacts in the museum and then assess whether they are protected from theft? Are they alarmed, or are the windows and walls strengthened?

> **SUGGESTIONS**
> - **MAKE** a 'Wanted' poster for an imaginary criminal that has managed to steal one or more of the museum's most valuable artefacts. Describe how the criminal and his accomplices managed to overcome the museum's security.
> - **MODEL** a replica of one of the museum's artefacts. Use clay, papier-mâché or cardboard for the structure before painting or colouring it. To make it look extra precious and shiny, add a layer of PVA glue as this is transparent when dry and acts like a varnish.

> **TIPS**
> - Visit during off-peak periods and you might be able to get cheaper entry or even free entry.
> - To keep costs down, take some homemade sandwiches and drinks with you.
> - Look at a plan or map of the museum and consider the areas of interest you want to see.

LEARNING AROUND
A CASTLE

Castles and forts have a mysterious lure for both young and old. A reconstructed or well-preserved historical building provides a wow factor from afar but the excitement begins inside! Castles are exciting because they are rich in history; they may contain grand halls adorned in impressive paintings and shiny armour or eery dungeons where gruesome deaths and tortures took place. The very spot that you stand on may have been the spot where a famous king marched into battle against an attacking enemy force.

BEFORE YOU GO...

Castles and forts can vary tremendously; some are immaculately kept and provide a full day out with captivating entertainment, whereas others can be disappointingly sparse or in a ruined state that provides little for the imagination. When planning a trip for a family, it is important to find a suitable castle that will suit the kids' interests. Many cities boast castles that are worthy of a visit and the countryside also offers a range of spectacular gems. Once you have located a castle, try to contextualise where it is; look at a local map or search Google Maps to find its location, then compare it with older maps. This may lead to discussions about how the landscape has changed and spark questions about why the castle was built there.

Larger, well-known castles are usually open throughout the year. If planning a visit, find out if there are any themed events or demonstrations planned – these often happen at the weekend or during school holidays/vacations. During busy times, it might be advisable to book ahead to avoid disappointment.

The main aim of the visit is for children to gain a personal insight into the location and get something educational out of it. Prior to the visit, generate lines of enquiry based on their interests; what do they want to find out? Encourage them to ask questions. An easier line of enquiry might begin with 'who, what, when and where...', whereas a more difficult one might begin with 'why?'.

ENCOURAGING LINES OF ENQUIRY

- When was the castle built?
- Who lived in the castle?
- What was kept inside the courtyard of the castle?
- How has the castle changed since it was built?
- Why was the castle built near a river?

WHILE YOU ARE THERE...

Once you have arrived, your aim is to answer the questions that the children have thought of and find opportunities to broaden and deepen their understanding of castles. You can do this in a variety of ways, suited to your children's needs and interests.

ENCOURAGING DIFFERENT WAYS TO LEARN

LISTEN to an audio tour or a special talk as you walk around a castle. Many castles offer guided tours. An expert guide will tell ..... you about the castle's history as you walk round together in a group. Alternatively, an audio tour might be on offer. This will allow you to follow a route and listen at your own pace. Audio tours are ideal for children who are unable to sustain concentration for long periods of time.

READ through the snippets of information that are always provided at a castle. Although usually aimed at adults, key facts can be gleaned and discussed. Some places also provide treasure trails aimed at children. The trails require them to follow clues and find out key information as they go.

LOOK carefully at the rooms in a castle that have been refurbished to recreate the original period style of the building. Such recreations make it easier for children to get a more accurate picture of what it would have looked like. Some castles also offer demonstrations or re-enactments of historical events, e.g. a jousting tournament, a trebuchet launch or a birds of prey demonstration.

Support active learners by letting them **TRY ON OUTFITS** and pretend to be the former inhabitants; walk around the walls pretending to be a guard, stopping to look through arrow slits; climb up the spiral steps in a turret; scramble up the moat as if attacking the castle.

The ambience of the castle can often stimulate the **SENSES**. Old furniture and polished armour not only are a visual feast but also provide interesting smells. Children are often discouraged from touching things when out and about, but some venues actively encourage children to discover through touch. This can provide a more memorable experience.

ODD ONE OUT – FIND THE FAKE FACT!

- The biggest castle in the world is Prague castle in the Czech Republic (570 x130m/1870 x 426ft).
- ✗ Castles didn't have toilets; the moat was the toilet.
- The first castles were made of stone.
- Castle staircases were always built to spiral clockwise.

BE BOLD

Ask questions or speak to three different people. You could ask a member of staff if they can provide you with interesting facts about the castle; you could order a drink or a snack or you could ask for directions.

WHEN YOU GET BACK...

After returning from the castle visit, it is important to consolidate the learning that took place and keep a spark of interest alight. Choose from a range of activities, as your child will naturally prefer some more than others. The enquiring mind does not have to stop after the trip. You can keep the discussion going when you get home.

SUGGESTIONS

- Try to **MAKE** something you've seen, e.g. castle walls, trebuchet, giant crossbow, portcullis.
- **WRITE** your own facts based on the visit. Test the rest of the family and see how much everyone can remember.
- **DRAW** and label something that you enjoyed learning about, e.g. the armour, coat of arms, castle wall.
- **PLAY** *Just a Minute* on castles (see explanation on page 11).

LEARNING AROUND
A RELIGIOUS BUILDING

Church, mosque, synagogue, Hindu temple, Gurdwara, shrine, chapel... the list isn't endless, but it is quite long. Wherever you choose to visit, for whatever reason, a trip to a religious building is likely to be a thought-provoking and interesting experience, something that will help a young person grasp the cultural and religious diversity of the world.

BEFORE YOU GO...

Different religions have different customs and traditions, and ways to behave in their religious buildings. It is particularly important to be aware of appropriate codes of dress and behaviour and to comply respectfully with them. Before you go, spend time familiarising yourself with the religion so that you know the protocol and take any extra clothing items you might need to wear on entering the building, e.g. headwear or cover-up clothing.

The reactions of very young children to new experiences can sometimes be a little hard to predict. People are aware of this and are generally most understanding, but do make an effort to explain to your children the desired behaviour you want them to display. The more your children understand this and the reasons why it is important, the more likely they are to conform. This is an important part of the learning process and a reason in itself to take children to places of religious and cultural diversity.

Religious buildings are also interesting from the outside, so remember to spend as much time as you can exploring the exterior and the grounds.

ENCOURAGING LINES OF ENQUIRY
- When and why was the religious building built?
- What can you learn about the religion from the outside of the building?
- What are the rules, customs and traditions associated with this particular religious building?
- What can you learn about the religion from the statues, sculptures and artwork on display?

WHILE YOU ARE THERE...

This is one visit during which you don't want to be rushing around and making a lot of noise, out of respect for the other visitors. So try to give the children things to focus on, e.g. a statue or a painting. Set them a challenge of moving around as stealthily as possible.

ENCOURAGING DIFFERENT WAYS TO LEARN

LISTEN very carefully to the sounds, stifled conversations or other muted noises, such as footsteps, made by people around you as they try to be as quiet as they can. It's hard being quiet! See if you can be silent!

Use your sense of **SMELL** to find a sensory spot in the building or outside. It could be a candle, incense stick, food or flowers in a garden. Find the strongest aromas and let your nose lead you. Then think about the smells. What is their source? Why are they created?

IDENTIFY your favourite piece of artwork on display and go back to study it. Stand and look at it as hard as you can, for as long as you can. Describe the picture in great detail to someone else and see if they can take you to that very picture. Talk about what the picture shows and why.

SKETCH four or five different parts of the building when inside, then draw the whole building from the outside.

SUGGESTIONS

- **DRAW** or paint, from memory, your favourite art piece from the visit.
- **RESEARCH** the kinds of food that might be served inside the building during a festival period, if appropriate, and try to make one of them.
- Give a short **TALK** to someone about your visit, maybe even give a talk to your classmates at school.

TIPS

- Have some money at hand so you can make a financial donation if appropriate.
- Keep young children in close control.
- Check if photography is allowed inside the building before you attempt to take any snaps.

LEARNING AROUND
AN HISTORICAL BUILDING

Learning about historical buildings might not seem exciting, but you will be surprised how interesting and stimulating a trip to an historic or prehistoric site can be. The key to unlocking this interest is knowledge. If you are forearmed with even just a little bit of knowledge about the building you are visiting, it will make a world of difference. Look at the era of the building or the style and methods of construction. Such knowledge will give you confidence and encourage curiosity in your children to interpret the building and its past.

BEFORE YOU GO...

Below are some of the ways in which you can prepare yourself and your young historians for a visit to an historical building.

Learn a little bit about the period in which the building was constructed; was it during one of the main historical eras? If it's a very old site, it might even be prehistoric. If you are not sure when it was built, look online, as there will no doubt be articles, images and posts about it. Once you know the era, talk and think about what else was happening at this time. Historical enquiry is about trying to interpret the past: to understand not only what happened but why it happened and what the consequences or knock-on effects were. You cannot get a full understanding of history without looking at the broader historical context surrounding a site or the building within it.

Significant historical buildings or sites are usually linked to famous people from history. Humans, by our very nature, are interested in people. There are weekly magazines and daily news reports that obsess about knowing who people are, what they do and how successful they are. The same applies to our interest in historical figures. Find out about some of the important people linked to the building you are going to visit; it will add an interesting dimension to your day.

Depending on your children's ages and stages, you might want to look out for an historical building that has grounds or gardens of some sort, one that offers some space to play for the young visitors to let off steam.

ENCOURAGING LINES OF ENQUIRY
- When was the building or site constructed, and by whom?
- What can we learn from the building's features and architecture?
- How and why has the building or site changed over time?
- What would it have been like to live in the building or site?

TIPS

- To keep the kids interested, break up the time spent indoors with plenty of time outdoors.
- Look out for special events like outdoor concerts, theatre productions and re-enactments.
- If there's a chronological route through the building, try to follow it. Otherwise, let the kids lead the way!

WHILE YOU ARE THERE...

Trudging around a building for hours and repeatedly reading out information will become tedious for children, so try to make the visit varied by introducing a mix of short, punchy activities. Of course, encouraging children to have sustained focus and interest is important, but if it looks like your young historian is getting bored, switch the focus.

ENCOURAGING DIFFERENT WAYS TO LEARN

Set your child the **TASK** of becoming your personal tour guide. Give them a period of time – vary this depending on their age – to find out about a part of the building: a room, perhaps. Next, ask them to guide the adults around it, giving them a mini tour. Offer to pay them, but only if the tour is good enough!

Give your child a voice recorder, or a smartphone that can **RECORD** audio notes, and set them the task of recording an audio note for each of the key areas of the building. Limit each note to one minute, though, so they can focus their thoughts.

FIND OUT the vital statistics of the building, or part of the building, such as the floor area, window area etc. Insist that the measurements are made in units appropriate to the historic era of the building. If you are not sure what units were used in the relevant period, find a member of staff and and ask them. Older or more-able children could be challenged to convert any non-standard units or imperial units into metric equivalents.

DETECT materials by looking for evidence of erosion or wear in the building. Look, too, for 'missing' materials such as wall or floor coverings, tiles etc. Think about why/how they have gone: decay, removal or vandalisation?

ODD ONE OUT – FIND THE FAKE FACT!

- Stonehenge is a circular megalithic monument built in prehistoric times.
- The Great Sphinx, a stunning example of ancient Egyptian architecture, is approximately 4500 years old.
- ✗ The Parthenon of Greece was the chief temple to Aphrodite, goddess of love and beauty.
- The Colosseum is Rome's largest amphitheatre.

BE BOLD

When a photograph is taken, the person operating the camera misses out. Help prevent this by offering to take the photograph for them. Be bold, be brave, be helpful.

WHEN YOU GET BACK...

Throughout history, people who were wealthy, powerful and significant often left behind a legacy of some sort, a kind of stamp or mark. This is often apparent when visiting historical sites and buildings. Use this to spark a discussion with your family about what mark or legacy they would like to leave behind, and ask them how they might go about achieving this.

SUGGESTIONS

- Imagine the building you have visited is up for sale and that you are the estate agent responsible for selling it. MAKE a 'Particulars' sheet for the property, complete with sketches and descriptions and dimensions of the building.
- Once you have learned the real story about the building, now ask the question 'What if?' and WRITE an alternative history, imagining that the course of history had followed a different path, one of your own choosing.
- Take or MAKE a map of the building or site, and draw a squared grid over it. Now list the map coordinates for each of the key areas/objects/features and see if someone can add labels by following the coordinates.

LEARNING AROUND
A COTTAGE INDUSTRY

So, what is a cottage industry? Well, for the purposes of this page, it is a small-scale industry carried out at home by family members using their own equipment. It may seem like quite a vague term, but essentially it refers to home-based manufacturing, as opposed to factory-based, and the creation of products that are marketed and sold by the maker him/herself. In historical terms, cottage industries came about when agricultural workers sought to make use of their time during the quieter winter months. The Industrial Revolution of the 19th century killed off the cottage-industry approach, but in recent years new technology, the internet and a desire for a work/life balance has led to a revival of cottage industries.

BEFORE YOU GO...

The first place to look for evidence of a cottage-industry past is your local area. The chances are there will have been small-scale domestic industrial activity in the past. It may have been basket or rug making, lace manufacturing, or the spinners, weavers and dyers who had been involved in the textiles industry. Starting in your locality will stimulate a strong interest within your child and create a connection with their local area, its heritage and its history. The learning that then takes place further afield – when you visit an area with a tradition in a different type of cottage industry, for instance – will be stronger, as the learner will have a local reference point to compare and contrast with.

When looking further afield, choose somewhere that will resonate with your child's interests; a fascination with fine textiles might take you to an area with a rich heritage and tradition of lace manufacturing and lacework, whereas a leaning towards getting hands-on and dirty might take you in search of pottery and metalwork.

As you learn about the history and traditions around the cottage industries it is important to relate the concept to the modern-day world. At a time when industry and manufacturing processes are highly complicated and technical, and almost everything is mass produced and factory-based, youngsters might be surprised to learn about the growing trend for people to work from home, often for themselves, so they may follow their passions and interests, in a modern revival of the cottage-industry model.

ENCOURAGING LINES OF ENQUIRY
- What evidence is there of cottage industry in the local area?
- In the average town market, how many different cottage industries are represented?
- What are the pros and cons of the cottage industry model?
- Can a cottage industry be mechanised?

WHILE YOU ARE THERE...

When visiting a craft fair, market or living museum, make it as tactile and hands-on as possible. If it's a food-based industry, encourage the kids to try as much as they can. For art and craft industries, encourage them to let their creativity loose. Not taking part isn't an option.

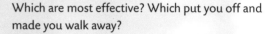

ENCOURAGING DIFFERENT WAYS TO LEARN

MAKE something! Cottage industry is all about the making, so find the kids' activity area, or a market stall encouraging people to have a go and, as the Nike motto says, 'Just Do It!'. What's the worst that can happen?

WATCH a demonstration of one of the more technical skill-based industries, like glass-blowing, or horseshoe making by a blacksmith. Get close and take in the aromas, feel the heat and don't be afraid to ask questions.

WALK the walk and **LISTEN** to people 'talk the talk'. It's no good making things if no one buys them, so being a salesperson is an important part of being a cottage-industry worker. Walk around the market paying attention to the sales approach and techniques used by the different stallholders.

Which are most effective? Which put you off and made you walk away?

Be **ECO SAVVY** by looking out for products that have been made from reused or recycled materials. Some people are really creative and literally turn waste and unwanted materials into desirable objects.

Get **ANALYTICAL** and categorise the cottage industries based on product type. Make up your own criteria such as: food, arty, gimmicky, useful... whatever you want!

LOOK at each cottage industry product through a magnifying glass – not literally, but try and investigate the products a bit more closely to identify the raw materials that have been used to make them.

ODD ONE OUT – FIND THE FAKE FACT!

- Nottingham is famous for the lace-making cottage industry.
- Shoe making was a popular cottage industry before the Industrial Revolution.
- ✗ The soft cheese manufacturing industry is known as the Cottage Cheese Cottage Industry.
- Many modern-day cottage industries have websites and online shops.

BE BOLD

Don't be afraid to barter when at a market. It's common practice overseas, and you've nothing to lose. Make sure you do it politely and respectfully and you might get yourself a bargain!

WHEN YOU GET BACK...

Creative entrepreneurial thinking, including problem-finding and problem-solving, and dynamism – making something happen – are key life skills/competences. Use the cottage industry model to stimulate in your children a taste of business by supporting and guiding them through a simple, small-scale entrepreneurial venture. You never know, you may even get a return on your investment.

SUGGESTIONS

Start your own cottage industry. Start small, like a lemonade stand in your front garden, or by making corn dolly 'offerings' for Valentine's Day. SELL your products for more than they cost you to make and then replenish your stock and start again, making a few more items than last time. You'll be surprised at how easy it is, so go on, give it a try.

PLACES TO GO

LEARNING AROUND
A Z●O

Zoos have changed a great deal over recent years. They are no longer places solely for 'entertainment' and novelty, but are more often centres of conservation and education. Zoos now play an important role in the upkeep of endangered animal species that are at risk of extinction. In fact, they work together as a coordinated global conservation community.

BEFORE YOU GO...

The zoo that you plan to visit is likely to have a particular specialism and breeding programmes, so do a bit of background research before you head out and encourage your young zoologists to go with some specific questions or things to find out. If they come home with their questions answered, then they will feel proud of themselves and this will make the visit more memorable.

One way to seek out the best information is to ask the various staff members directly or even a zookeeper him/herself. Preparing a series of questions in a notebook, with an idea of who might be the best person to ask them, is great preparation.

But make sure there is also plenty of 'slack' time for your children to enjoy. You may well be visiting a top-notch zoo, but that doesn't mean that the play area or gift shop won't also have a strong appeal for your children.

ENCOURAGING LINES OF ENQUIRY

- What are the different jobs that need fulfilling in order to run a zoo? What might be the training implications for the different roles?
- How do zoos provide for animals that in the wild would live in a range of different habitats?
- How do zoos attract customers?

WHILE YOU ARE THERE...

Visiting a zoo might be the only time your children and you are able to see exotic animals that would otherwise be in the wild. Treat the visit as a wildlife adventure, listening to and watching animals from around the world.

ENCOURAGING DIFFERENT WAYS TO LEARN

LISTEN to the noises that the animals make and find out what they mean. See how accurately you can imitate different animals. On the way home in the car, take it in turns to make an animal noise and see who can identify it.

LOOK at the amount of space each animal has. How have they tried to recreate the natural habitat?

WATCH the animals being fed. How do they behave? Is it natural? How has the zoo tried to make the enclosures seem as 'wild' as possible for the animals?

FILM some video footage of a favourite animal. Think like a film-maker, i.e. look to get some close-ups and some distance shots that show a range of activity and emotions.

SUGGESTIONS

- **EDIT** the video clips into a documentary-style film that includes some voice-over narration giving facts and information. The film might try to emulate a David Attenborough or a Steve Backshall Deadly 60 recording.
- **DEBATE** whether zoos are good or bad/cruel. Find evidence. Create a pros and cons list. Ask other visitors what they think.
- **COMBINE** two animals together to create a new species. What would they eat? Where would they live? Create a fact file using this information.

TIPS

- To avoid information overload, vary the experience by listening to talks and watching displays as well as reading information signs and speaking to other people.
- Make sure all safety guidance and signs are read and understood by the children, particularly those that deal with how to behave around the animal enclosures.

LEARNING AROUND
A CAMPSITE

Campsites and caravan sites are great places for families to enjoy whatever the weather, contrary to what some people might think. Admittedly, camping is not so much fun if you are wet and cold, but this really only indicates that you were not properly prepared in the first place. There's no such thing as bad weather, just the wrong clothing! Your tent also needs to be up to the task too; more about that later.

Your children will be sure to love their outdoor time and the excitement of snuggling up in a sleeping bag. Expose them to the joys of camping when they are young and they will grow up with an ability to enjoy and appreciate the simple things in life.

BEFORE YOU GO...

Preparation is an important consideration for the success of this trip, so, in the words of Lord Baden-Powell: 'Be Prepared!' He knew a thing or two about the outdoors after all. To start you off, create a kit list with the kids. Well, multiple kit lists in fact: one for each person attending the trip; one for the hardware – tent, pegs, stove etc; and one for the food and drink. By making sure you have everything you need on-site you'll give yourself a better chance of having the best time possible; a happy camper is a warm, dry and well-fed camper.

Now it's time to look into the site and area you are visiting in more detail. Is there a stream or river nearby? Will you have access to a beach or forest? Look online, but also consider buying a large-scale map of the site and surrounding area, as this will give you something to use when you are there, as well as an opportunity for planning activities in advance, such as shelter building, making bow and arrows or marking a cycle route.

And if you need to 'sell' the notion of a night under canvas to your children, tell them you're going to take all of their favourite outdoor play equipment including the football, Swingball and Nerf guns! Not forgetting the rounders equipment or the baseball bat, of course – these are must-haves for every camping trip.

ENCOURAGING LINES OF ENQUIRY
- How is the campsite organised? How much area is there for each pitch?
- Is the campsite open all year round? If so, why and how is it kept open? If not, why not?
- Where is the best place to camp for different needs: A Family? An older couple? A group of teenagers?

WHILE YOU ARE THERE...

One of the most important things you can do as a parent is step back and let the kids explore and discover this new and exciting environment. Then set them challenges to do – with or without you – and get them to report back on their progress. Check out the ideas below.

ENCOURAGING DIFFERENT WAYS TO LEARN

Big Business? Think of the campsite as a business, because that is what it is in reality, and **EVALUATE** it in terms of outgoings; look at the costs of buying a field, paying a cleaner and upkeep, together with income (payment received from the owners of tents and caravans). Consider the length of the holiday season. A campsite may only operate during the spring and summer months – and what happens if someone books but doesn't show up? With the facts and figures at hand, justify whether a campsite is big business or not.

LOOK at all the tent, caravan and awning designs. How are the different tents constructed? This is done more easily by watching someone put up or take down a tent. Tally up the colours of the tents to determine which one is the most popular for family tents, small two-man tents or caravan awnings.

LISTEN to the sounds of the site and create a Campsite Sound Profile. This is a kind of bar chart, with each bar showing the sounds that are made at different times of the day. Make up an arbitrary scale and don't worry about it being too accurate, just try to record the main patterns and causes of noise.

PLAY Use the outdoor play equipment you and any friends have brought along to make an outdoor exercise circuit. Get all the adults to complete the circuit each day you are at the site; tell them they will feel better for it!

ODD ONE OUT – FIND THE FAKE FACT!

- ✗ Wild camping is illegal in England, Scotland and Wales.
- Nomads in the Sahara live in tents of woven goat and camel hair.
- Climbers use portaledges (hanging tents) to sleep in when scaling large cliff faces.
- Campers can buy tree tents, which are suspended between two tree trunks.

BE BOLD

Go up to a child of a similar age to you and ask them if they want to play with you – it could be the start of a new friendship.

WHEN YOU GET BACK...

One practical – and not very glamorous – thing you must do when you return home is air out your gear: tent, flysheet, sleeping bags etc. Any fabric-based item could rot if left in a damp state. It's easy to put it off and 'do it later' but the chances are you'll forget and the result could be mouldy or even rotten equipment!

SUGGESTIONS

- **DESIGN** a new tent, using your observations. Concentrate on a specific market, e.g. a family or a backpacker. Draw the tent from the front and side, and create a plan view, too. Give your tent a funky name to attract the attention of customers.
- **CAMP** out in your garden or even make a shelter. Try camping in sub-zero conditions – you can always nip indoors if you get too chilly.
- **WRITE** or **EMAIL** any friends you have made at the site. You never know, you may have found a new friend for life!

LEARNING AROUND
AN OUTDOOR RETAIL PARK

We are all familiar with the concept of a retail park: the homogenous-looking developments that live on the fringes of our cities and towns, each with the same generic formula of big-box chain retailers, complete with the occasional supermarket and its discount fuel. But look at them with outdoor learning in mind and you may just see them in a different light.

BEFORE YOU GO...

On this occasion leave your wallet or purse behind because this trip to the mall won't cost you anything. The idea behind this visit is to learn about location, human geographical patterns and time, along with people and space management. Now doesn't that sound a lot more interesting than going shopping?

Out-of-town retail parks are exactly that, located away from a town. You won't find them in the traditional town centres and there are reasons for this which ought to be explored before you visit. Much of this prior understanding can be gained by probing and prompting with questions like: 'If the rent for a house costs more in the city centre, how might this transfer to fringe land on the outskirts?' Or 'Traffic and parking in towns and cities is a real issue isn't it? Why and what are the issues?'.

With a grasp of some of the positive influencers in support of retail parks, you can head out to your local mall or park with a bit of knowledge and a list of other factors to explore.

ENCOURAGING LINES OF ENQUIRY

- What diversity of shops and products are on sale at the retail park? How does that compare to a different retail park?
- What are the shopping patterns of people that visit a retail park?
- How is the parking organised? And what measures have been put in place for busy, congested times?

WHILE YOU ARE THERE...

To get a good sense of how retail parks are used, focus on different areas and times of the day. Go with a focus such as: how long do people spend in a retail park? Does the duration of time that people spend at the park relate to the shops they visit?

ENCOURAGING DIFFERENT WAYS TO LEARN

WATCH and **STUDY** people's visits to enable you to assess people's shopping habits, e.g. five out of ten people studied spent less than 30 minutes at the retail park, or people generally park nearest the first shop they visit.

TALK to people to find out which shops they visited to establish which are the most/least popular. The reasons why may be deduced, e.g. online shopping of electrical goods is on the increase so electrical superstores may be less popular than they were when the park was built.

COUNT the number of car-parking spaces and capture a rough percentage of free space available in the car park at key parts of the day: opening, lunchtime, closing, after hours.

CAPTURE a stop-motion photo of the car park every 10 minutes. Combine the images into a short stop-motion animation to show traffic flow.

MONITOR the number of single-use plastic bags that come out of the retail park.

SUGGESTIONS

- **CREATE** an infographic (a visual representation) of the data you have collected. Try to include all of the themes and trends you've observed.
- **LOBBY** the managers of each of the shops in the retail park about the number of single-use plastic bags that customers take away on an average day, asking them to do something to reduce the quantities.
- **LIST** and explain the negative issues around retail parks, such as pollution, taking trade away from town centres, lack of choice etc.

TIPS

- Visit the same retail park at different times of the day to get a fuller picture of how they function.
- Take a clipboard with you as this helps response-gathering and data collection while out and about.

LEARNING AROUND
A RACECOURSE

For the most part of any given year a racecourse will be unused, as race meets are not very frequent. This makes them easily accessible and they are valuable places at which to learn, have fun and even get some exercise . You don't even have to be there *'furlong'*!

BEFORE YOU GO...

Children might not be too aware of the sport of horse racing, so it is a good idea to try and look at some photos or video on the internet or on TV to help them to relate to the course when they get there, and to understand what a course will be like on a race day.

Through looking at imagery, children will be able to glean a lot, and it is this initial engagement with the sport that will lead to some interesting lines of enquiry, excitement and anticipation for the visit itself.

For older children it is appropriate to introduce the notion of gambling and how the whole sport of horse racing is built upon people willing to bet money on whether they think a horse will win or not – a risk that is weighed up by a study of 'form' for both horse and jockey.

ENCOURAGING LINES OF ENQUIRY
- What are the common features of racecourses?
- How are racecourses designed to keep the public, the horses and jockeys safe?
- What evidence is there of sponsorship and what does this tell you about the sport and the people that are interested in it?

WHILE YOU ARE THERE...

Visiting a racecourse on race day will be an exciting and atmospheric experience. While the intention of a visit is not to encourage gambling or even condone horse racing as a sport, getting caught up in the thrill of the race will be difficult to avoid.

ENCOURAGING DIFFERENT WAYS TO LEARN

LISTEN On a race day the noise levels around the course will vary dramatically. Try and log all of the sounds, from the horses' hooves to the cheering of excited 'punters' as they encourage their horse to victory. Encourage your youngster to listen to a race from start to finish, with their ear on the ground.

Explore the **SMELLS** of a racecourse and map them. Which areas smell the worst or nicest? Why is that?

OBSERVE the horses as they parade before a race and then during a race. Look at the people around the course and the outfits they wear, from jockeys in their colours to security and marshals, to the general public. On some race meets people really dress up and even wear fancy hats.

GET ACTIVE on a non-race day by getting the youngsters to walk or run round the racecourse, as if they are racing horses. They will really appreciate the scale of the place.

SUGGESTIONS
- **INVESTIGATE** whether racing is a good thing or bad thing for horses and then try and persuade someone of your viewpoint.
- **DESIGN** a range of jockey outfits that you would like to wear if you were a jockey.
- **THINK** of ways that the racecourse could be used by the local community when the racecourse is not holding a race event, so it could benefit from the place.

TIPS
- Try and visit a racecourse twice: on a race day and on a non-race day.
- Visit as many different parts of the course as you can.
- Consider the pros and cons of a town having a racecourse.

LEARNING AROUND
A MARKET

Markets, big and small, are held all over the world. The venues, often located in the centre of a town or city, provide a meeting point for people to buy and sell produce. The word 'market' originates from the Latin *mercatus* and *mercari*, which means to trade.

A general market often sells a wide variety of produce and is a central hub of activity in a town. Some markets specialise in certain types of produce such as fish, flowers, antiques and food. Farmers' markets are becoming increasingly popular as people search out locally grown produce rather than being reliant upon larger supermarkets.

Christmas time is when the choice increases, as visiting markets from around the world treat us to new festive delights. These are worth visiting in order to broaden the horizons and get a taste (literally and metaphorically) of what they have to offer.

BEFORE YOU GO...

The market square, also known as a place, piazza or plaza in other languages, is a feature of many towns. It is the traditional location where market stalls are set up on market day. The buildings that surround the market square frame it and put it into context.

When deciding which market to visit, select one that will provide an interesting setting and will sell produce that appeals to all family members. If visiting a market that specialises in one particular piece of produce, you might need to carry out a bit of research beforehand, e.g. find out the names of some flowers, where certain fish are from or create a 'To Find' list: challenge each other to find up to 10 items from the list at the market.

Markets tend to vary from place to place, so before setting off, check out the times and days to avoid disappointment. Timing your visit is quite important; a visit near the end of the day is when bargains can be found, as stallholders begin to pack up and are keen for a quick sale.

Markets are steeped in history. They existed in ancient times; the Ancient Greeks held agoras and the Romans held forums. When visiting a market, find out how far back it dates. How has it changed over the years?

ENCOURAGING LINES OF ENQUIRY
- Where is the market located in the town?
- Where does the produce come from?
- How much does it cost to hire a pitch on the market?
- How old are the buildings that surround the market?
- For how long has a market been held in the town. Has its location changed over time?
- How do the different stallholders try to sell their wares?

TIPS

- Take money, including change, with you.
  It will be quicker and easier to pay with cash.
  Many market stalls don't accept card payments.
- Take along some bags to put your purchases
  in – avoid collecting lots of plastic bags.

WHILE YOU ARE THERE...

Markets are full of character: not only the characters within them, but also the character of the town. Spend time wandering around to soak up the atmosphere – the sights, sounds and smells of the place. Take in the bigger picture before beginning to look at individual stalls.

ENCOURAGING DIFFERENT WAYS TO LEARN

TALK to some stallholders and find out where they get their produce from, how far they have travelled and how long their day is.

WALK around the market and map out its layout in your head – you could use paper if it helps. Could it be organised better? How would you organise it?

SEARCH for produce. Make a list of things that are on sale at the market and challenge other members of the family to find them. Turn it into a competition to see who can find the most unusual items.

LOOK at the price of what is on sale. Compare the prices between two or more stalls. What is the price difference? Which stall offers the best deals?

BARTER with a stallholder. Bartering involves negotiating with the stallholder over the price of an item. In some countries you are expected to barter over the price before buying anything.

ODD ONE OUT – FIND THE FAKE FACT!

- At floating markets produce is sold from boats.
- ✗ Flea markets sell fleas and other insects.
- In Arabic a market is called a 'souk'.
- One of the oldest and largest markets in the world is the Grand Bazaar in Istanbul.

BE BOLD

Barter with a stallholder. See how much you can get off an item that you wish to buy. Alternatively, see if you can get a cheaper price if you buy more than one of something.

WHEN YOU GET BACK...

Expand your interest and knowledge of markets by looking at other examples around the world. Find out where is there a night market, a floating market or a wet market.

SUGGESTIONS

- **MAKE** something from what you buy, e.g. a smoothie from the fruits you bought. Turn it into your own enterprise and set up your own market stall selling your product.
- **RESEARCH** other markets around the world. How do they compare to the one you visited? What are they famous for?
- Visit another market and **COMPARE** it to the one you've seen. What are the similarities/differences?
- Look at paintings of markets. **DRAW OR PAINT** your own market scene.

LEARNING AROUND
A PLAYGROUND

Next time you visit a playground, have a good lark about alongside your children before engaging them in some activities that will get them thinking. Learning and play, do they really go together? You bet.

You will also be sure to enjoy the added feel-good benefits of being active in the outdoors, even if the weather is not being a good sport.

BEFORE YOU GO...

Once you start thinking creatively about making opportunities for learning that could take place in a playground, you'll be amazed at just how many ideas you'll have.

For example, the playground is the perfect place to see science in action: gravity tries to constantly pull you to the ground; friction tries to slow you down or make your hands and knees sore; and there are forces associated with spinning, both centrifugal and centripetal.

Playgrounds are also great places for capturing and harnessing children's imaginations. Children will know what their local playground looks like, but let them loose on Google to find out about 'the most amazing' or the 'world's best' playground. Get them to think about what makes a playground appealing. Print off a picture for them to take and make comparisons with your local playground.

Wherever you go and whatever you do, make sure there are plenty of activities that involve play, fun and thinking going on. Kids aren't spending enough time outdoors these days, so time spent at a playground is time well spent.

ENCOURAGING LINES OF ENQUIRY
- What sort of play does a playground encourage?
- Are playgrounds made to be too safe? Why the emphasis on safety?
- How natural is a playground – in design, the activities it promotes and the materials used to create it?

WHILE YOU ARE THERE...

As parents we tend to interfere too much – we can't help it. On this occasion let the kids run wild. Let them try all the equipment and play. After all, it is a PLAYground! Even when you introduce the activities, take a step back – try not to hover.

....

ENCOURAGING DIFFERENT WAYS TO LEARN

To encourage an understanding of the centrifugal force, place soft items on a roundabout and then begin to spin it. See how long it needs to spin for and how fast it gets before your item gets thrown off.

Playgrounds naturally encourage **PHYSICAL** activities from climbing, pulling, pushing and running, so use these to your benefit. Create a circuit-training route that uses the playground equipment creatively to exercise different parts of the body.

Take a step back and **OBSERVE** what is happening at the playground. Set a hypothesis, such as 'the roundabout is the most popular piece of equipment'. Prove this wrong or right by collecting data. Create a tally of how many people went on the different equipment during a set period of time.

EVALUATE how accessible the playground is for children with accessibility issues, such as: How wheelchair-friendly is the park and its equipment? How easily could a child with impaired vision safely negotiate the space?

MEASURE how much each piece of playground equipment affects heart rate by taking a pulse reading and breath count before and after one minute of using each piece of equipment. What deductions can be made from the results?

SUGGESTIONS

- **CREATE** an outdoor fitness circuit in your garden and then challenge all of your family members to complete it. You could even take their pulse and breathing rates before and after, then comment on their fitness.
- **WRITE** to a local government councillor or officer to give your comment on how accessible you found the playground to be. Be polite, fair and honest, and remember to back up your comments with examples.

TIPS

- Depending on the location of the playground, you might need to consider activities that could take place of an evening, so be aware and observant of broken glass and other possible dangers.
- If there isn't a fence around the playground, a quick check for dog waste might avoid any messy incidents.

LEARNING AROUND
A WIND FARM

Whether you love them or hate them, wind farms and other kinds of renewable 'green' energy are here to stay – whatever the weather. But whether you are in favour of them or not, why not get out to visit one. Talk to the people there and find out about the role of the wind farm for our increasingly overpopulated and energy-deprived planet.

BEFORE YOU GO...

Some of the world's largest wind farms are made up of hundreds of individual turbines covering tens of square miles/kilometres, generating thousands of megawatts of power. More common are smaller farms consisting of just a small handful of turbines, sometimes only three or four.

Regardless of the number of individual turbines on a wind farm, they all work on the same principle: using wind power to generate electricity. Since turbines are powered by wind, it is a source of renewable energy that has important 'green' credentials.

A visit to a wind farm and the sense of enormity of these giant windmill structures is guaranteed to fascinate the most sceptical of people. Children will certainly find the size of the turbines awesome. Some may find the noise surprising, others still may consider the structures beautiful and elegant.

Tap into local perception and there will be a significant body of people that do not like wind turbines at all; well, not in their own backyards that is. Resistance to wind farms can be strong – hurricane strength, in fact.

ENCOURAGING LINES OF ENQUIRY
- Are wind turbines bad for wildlife, particularly birds?
- Do more people like wind farms than dislike them?
- How large are wind turbines?
- What are the parts of a wind turbine?
- How do wind turbines work?

TIPS

- Take with you a cross-section picture of a turbine to help with visualising the innards of the turbine.
- Get the children to imagine electrical cables below the ground that carry the electricity from the turbines into the National Grid, via a substation.

WHILE YOU ARE THERE...

While you are choosing a wind farm to visit, try and find one that allows you to get really close to the turbines themselves, just so you can experience the full scale of them – they are huge! This in itself will make the learning memorable. Even better, visit a wind farm on an open day or write to the operators of the farm and ask them to give the family a tour of the facility.

ENCOURAGING DIFFERENT WAYS TO LEARN

LISTEN to points for and against a wind farm. One of the arguments aimed at wind farms by people that don't support their existence is that they are noisy. Take this opportunity to find out first-hand just how noisy they are. Using a smartphone, take recordings using a voice recorder app at various distances away from the turbines.

TALK to local people and ask them questions. The best way to tap into the local community's perception of a wind farm is to check out their opinions. Try to speak to as many people as possible; a short, two-question survey is better than a long one. Understand what a NIMBY is.

GET PHYSICAL. Find out how tall a wind turbine is and pace out this distance on the ground using strides. This will provide a concrete reference of just how large the structures are. Get the children to close their eyes and then turn slowly until they feel the wind blowing directly onto their faces. When they open their eyes they should be facing in the same direction as each other– and all of the turbines.

Encourage children to **LOOK** closely at the shape and design of the turbine blades. They are not flat like the sails of a windmill but more like the propeller of an aeroplane. Encourage them to notice the direction in which the turbines are facing (all in the same direction). With a timer, measure the speed of the turbine blades. Do they always spin at the same speed?

ODD ONE OUT – FIND THE FAKE FACT!

✗ Bats can avoid turbine blades.
• On blustery days, wind turbines can spin so fast that they explode.
• Birds sometimes fly into the turbine blades and die.
• Not all wind turbines are white.

BE BOLD

Challenge your youngsters to phone up a wind power company to find out whether wind turbines are harmful to wildlife.

THE INNER WORKINGS OF A WIND TURBINE

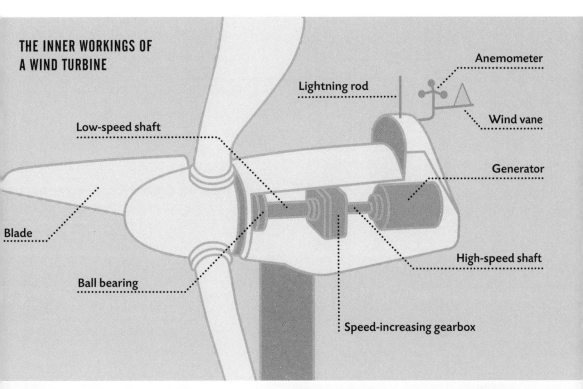

Anemometer

Lightning rod

Wind vane

Low-speed shaft

Generator

Blade

High-speed shaft

Ball bearing

Speed-increasing gearbox

WHEN YOU GET BACK...

For this visit, many initial lines of enquiry may still be unanswered when you return home. This will require the kids to partake in some research and information gathering.

SUGGESTIONS

• Carry out **RESEARCH** into the unanswered lines of enquiry. There is a lot of information on the internet.
• **PRESENT** your findings (using one wildlife example and one piece of local perception) to the company that owns the wind turbine – they will value it.
• **ILLUSTRATE** a cross-section view of a turbine.
• **MAKE** a windmill like those on sale at seaside shops. What is the best blade/sail shape?

LEARNING AROUND
A VILLAGE

This project and the two that follow – Town and City – are closely related in terms of the areas that they cover and are designed to give a young learner a deeper understanding of the human settlements we live in and/or travel through on a regular basis.

BEFORE YOU GO...

If you already live in a village, then you might want to think about visiting a different village in your area, or a village in another county... or even in a different country. Or you could simply learn about your own village; it doesn't matter really, because the tasks you will be engaged in will probably not be ones you have tended to do already.

Taking stock of what your child knows about what a village is may be a good starting point. They may have heard of and even use the term, but what do they think it means? You will probably elicit something like 'it is small and has people living in it' which is true, but needs further clarification. Talking about villages might bring about the term 'hamlet', which also may need clarifying. In Britain, a hamlet is smaller than a village and doesn't have a church, for instance.

Once you have identified the level of your child's understanding, make it your aim to consolidate and further it during your visit.

ENCOURAGING LINES OF ENQUIRY
- What makes a village a village and not a hamlet, town or city?
- Is the village thriving, stagnating or dying? What are the reasons for this?
- What are the pros and cons of living in a village?

WHILE YOU ARE THERE...

Villages are small places so try and park up somewhere central so that you can have a good walk around the entire village. Make this a bit more appealing for the kids by letting them cycle around.

ENCOURAGING DIFFERENT WAYS TO LEARN

WALK around the village and look at the street names to see what you can learn about the village's past.

SOUNDSCAPE Close your eyes and listen to the sounds around you. Visualise in your imagination a picture to go with them. As you continue to listen, paint a composite image of the village. Open your eyes; how does the view compare?

COUNT or **ESTIMATE** the number of houses in the village. Use the map printouts you have to help you with this. Use this to estimate the approximate number of village residents.

SPEAK to a local and ask them to list all of the services the village has, such as a post office, shops, a doctor's surgery etc. Ask them if the village has always had these services or was there once more or less? The answer to these questions will give an indication of whether the village is thriving or dying.

ASSESS how active the village community is by looking at the village notice board. Find out what's on and how varied the events on offer are.

PLAY on the village playground. How does it compare to your local playground?

SUGGESTIONS

- Give the village a health check report based on how many services it has, how active the village community is and what condition the buildings are in etc. **MAKE** a simple checklist with a summary of thriving/stagnant/dying.
- **DEBATE** with a family member what the pros and cons are of living in a village: nice views versus lack of facilities; quiet roads and streets versus boring and not much to do.

TIPS

- Try and tap into the vibe of the village by engaging with the locals.
- Print out a couple of Google Maps to show road and satellite views before you go.
- Point out issues like holiday-let properties and the concept of second homes and their impact.

LEARNING AROUND
A **TOWN**

This activity is the second of three that aims to give a young learner a deeper understanding of the human settlements we live and/or travel through – the other two associated projects are Village (page 56) and City (page 60). Each page can stand alone or be used as a series.

BEFORE YOU GO...

Towns by their very nature are often quite big places with lots of services, amenities and history; this makes them interesting places to visit. The motivation for your visit to a chosen town will depend on what it has to offer. Whether your visit is to see an historical feature, learn about an historical event, or simply to experience the retail opportunities or attend a leisure event, go with a clear focus or intention. Also, make sure you all come back after the visit with a clearer understanding of what differentiates a town from a village or a city.

As with any learning experience, and before you try and extend a learner's understanding, it's important to establish what they already know about the subject. One way to do this is by playing the game *Just a Minute*, where players have to speak for 60 seconds on a topic without hesitation, deviation or repetition. Choose the topic 'Towns' or 'The town of XXX' and see how confidently each family member can speak for a limited time.

ENCOURAGING LINES OF ENQUIRY
- What makes a town what it is (and not a village or a city)?
- How well connected is the town?
- What services and amenities can be found?
- Is the town more like a city or a village?

WHILE YOU ARE THERE...

Because the notion of what a town is can be quite hard to define – it is not simply a case of how big or populous a settlement is – get out and about with the locals; talk to them, ask them questions and listen to their stories.

ENCOURAGING DIFFERENT WAYS TO LEARN

SURVEY the locals as they wander around in their lunch break and ask about where they work; make a tally. Try to establish whether the majority of people work in manufacturing, the service industry or commerce. This is one of the ways that a town can be defined.

VISIT some of the important buildings such as the town hall and council buildings. Speak to the staff about the governing powers the council has and how it represents the people.

RIDE any form of public transport – train, bus or tram – to see the different areas of the town. Try to classify them as you go around into types of activity: residential, retail, industrial, commercial or business.

LISTEN to the town centre. Find the centre and close your eyes. What can you hear? Categorise the noises into: human, mechanical, transport, animals and birds. Who/what makes the most noise?

Use a map to **COUNT** the A roads, B roads, waterways, railways and cycle routes to get a grasp of how well connected the town is.

SPEAK to someone from the town who is of retirement age about how the town has changed over the years.

SUGGESTIONS

- When you get home, **REPLAY** the game *Just a Minute* – it should be easier to speak more knowledgeably about the topic now.
- **COMPARE** the sizes of towns on Google maps. Does size really matter?
- **RESEARCH** a town in a contrasting locality or even country. Create an information sheet for this town, and the one you have visited, to see how they compare. Find out what the main similarities and differences are, and then tell someone about them.

TIPS

- Try to travel around the town on foot and/or public transport.
- Speak to people about the town they live in.
- Visit important buildings like the town hall or council buildings.
- Seek out the tourist information centre.

LEARNING AROUND
A CITY (AND CAPITAL CITIES)

This project is the third of three that aims to help develop an understanding of human settlements big and small. It can be used as a stand-alone resource or in conjunction with that of the Village (page 56) and the Town (page 58) projects.

BEFORE YOU GO...

If a lack of clarity exists over what constitutes a village or a town, then the same applies to a city, particularly in some countries around the world. In the UK, the ability to up the status of a town to a city is held by the monarch, having taken advice from government ministers. Size does matter: a city needs to be home to over 300,000 people, but it is also important for it to have a distinct identity that is at the centre of a wider area.

A capital city, or 'head' city, is easily defined as the city in which the national government is housed and the place that normally acts as the administrative centre for the country concerned.

If you are heading out to a capital city, make sure you visit the buildings where the government is based, as well as other important buildings associated with the city and country's administration. There may also be important buildings in other cities to make a visit worthwhile, so check out which locations within a city will appeal to you and your family.

> ### ENCOURAGING LINES OF ENQUIRY
> * What specialised functions does a city have to offer?
> * Where is the city sited? Why is that?
> * What problems exist in cities?
> * What are green belts and why do they exist?

WHILE YOU ARE THERE...

As you walk and travel around the city, draw attention to significant buildings that house important functions, such as: a large hospital, an important sports venue, a theatre, a city university or a religious building or museum. Also point out the hustle and bustle and the cosmopolitan multi-ethnic feel of the place or the greater choice of restaurants and shops.

ENCOURAGING DIFFERENT WAYS TO LEARN

LISTEN to the sounds of the city. Compare this to the sounds, or lack of them, heard in the village and even the town centre.

FEEL the vibrations of the traffic, trains and underground transport system.

PLAY a game of football or rounders in one of the city's green belt areas to experience the benefits that they offer. Count the number of sports or types of activity taking place (joggers or dog walkers, for example) and appreciate how important green areas are for city dwellers.

CATCH as many different forms of transport as you can during your visit. A city offers a range of transport options, including some unusual and quirky modes, such as tuk-tuks, pedal-powered taxis and horse-drawn carriages.

TAKE photos of some of the negative aspects of cities such as road congestion, pollution, damage to buildings or overcrowding, as well as positive aspects such as regular public transport and many exciting places for entertainment and leisure.

FIND a view of the city from on-high. Either visit an attraction like a big wheel or a building viewpoint, or find your own high point. Go high enough to be able to see the urban sprawl.

SUGGESTIONS

- **PRINT**, cut out and stick the photographs you have taken onto two pieces of paper labelled 'City: Good Points' and 'City: Bad Points'. Does the balance of your photos reflect your thoughts about cities?
- Do some **RESEARCH** into cities and their populations to prove/disprove this statement: Capital cities always have the largest populations.
- **MAKE** a map for a 'City of your Dreams' and once you have included all of the amenities and services you think it should have, name it – after yourself, of course.

TIPS

- Get hold of a city map to help you orientate and navigate your way around.
- Tourist bus tours offer a good way to see the important sites and functions of a city.
- Buy a one-day travel card to enable you to hop on and off local transport as you explore the regions of the city.

LEARNING AROUND
ALLOTMENTS AND GARDENS

Gardens come in all shapes and sizes. Their design and uses vary tremendously: some gardens provide a practical space for nearby residents, some are purely ornamental; others are used for producing food. We usually associate gardens with the patch of ground attached to a house, but increasingly modern houses have less and less space for gardens.

Allotments are small parcels of land that form part of a communal plot. Budding gardeners often hire allotments, for which they pay a membership fee or an annual rent to use the land.

Gardening, whether in a garden, allotment, vegetable patch or window box, is an increasingly popular and educational hobby. It is a fun and rewarding activity that develops an understanding about cause and effect through investigation; an ability to reason and discover the science of plants; physical activity that is productive; and a love of nature.

BEFORE YOU GO...

You won't have to travel far for this learning opportunity; if you have a garden, you simply need to step outside. If you don't have a garden, try to visit a friend, family member or neighbour's garden or allotment; get them involved and ask if you can help, or better still have a small space of your own for growing. You don't need to be an expert gardener; in fact, more learning may take place through curiosity and experimentation.

There are plenty of scientific learning opportunities around gardening. Your budding horticulturists will develop the skills to grow plants, care for wildlife and nurture a love for the outdoors. This project will take time of course, since plants need time to grow.

Before getting out and dirty, take some time to understand the decision-making and planning involved in growing plants. Learn about the types of soils in which certain plants grow best and find

out which type of soil your garden has. Visit a garden centre to look at the variety of seeds on offer. You can also ask any questions and seek advice from the experts there.

Decide whether or not you are going to take an organic approach to your gardening. Find out what it means to produce organic or non-organic produce and the impact that it has on both the plants and the environment.

ENCOURAGING LINES OF ENQUIRY
- What soil type does your garden or allotment have?
- What considerations need to be made when choosing which plants to grow?
- How much time needs to be dedicated to gardening?
- Which plants grow well together?
- How often should you rotate crops?

TIPS

- Have some useful tools at hand, such as a trowel, garden fork and gloves.
- Supervise young children when using tools.
- Ensure that children do not eat any unknown plants.

WHILE YOU ARE THERE...

Rather than a single trip, this learning opportunity should ideally take place at regular intervals through the year. The time of year will affect what can and should be done.

ENCOURAGING DIFFERENT WAYS TO LEARN

Go on a **SENSORY** walk. Use your senses to explore a garden: take in the different smells, such as mint and flowers; textures such as woolly lamb's ears plants or spiky thistles; and the shapes and colours of the plants; as well as the sounds of the wildlife. You could even taste some of the fruit, vegetables or herbs – children should always check with an adult first.

MAKE a wormery and watch these fascinating wriggly things turn plant waste into soil before your very eyes. Look online for instructions on how to do this.

FIND OUT why leaves are green. Cover a leaf on a plant with black paper. Return a couple of days later to see what has happened. You might need to do a bit of research to find out why.

FIND OUT where plants grow best. Plant seeds in different places in the garden and see which grows the fastest and looks healthy. Why?

HELP out the insects. Gardens rely on insects to help pollinate the plants and some predatory insects act as natural pest control so plant a wildflower area and keep your insects happy with a hibernation hotel. See online for ideas.

MAKE a scarecrow to keep the birds away from your vegetables. Birds are clever creatures, so think about what you could do to keep one step ahead of them.

PHOTOGRAPH your garden in different seasons to show how it changes through the year.

GET PHYSICAL and do some digging. Mix in manure to give the soil nutrients for growing, or dig up the vegetables you've managed to grow.

MEASURE the area of different allotments. Who has the biggest plot?

GROW your own vegetables. This will take time and effort, but you will enjoy the rewards.

ODD ONE OUT – FIND THE FAKE FACT!

- ✗ You cannot eat the flowers from a nasturtium plant.
- Tomatoes are in the same family as potatoes.
- Carrots can be orange, purple, white, yellow and red.
- Sunflowers move throughout the day in response to the movement of the sun.

BE BOLD

- Enter something that you've grown into a local horticultural competition. You never know, you might win a prize.
- Donate vegetables that you've grown to local people who might benefit from your kindness.

WHEN YOU GET BACK...

Since this project will involve multiple visits, follow up the learning with indoor projects that will complement the outdoor activity each time you return. Gardening doesn't only have to happen outdoors.

SUGGESTIONS

- **MAKE** something with the vegetables that you grow, such as a salad or some soup.
- **RUN A COMPETITION** with friends, family and neighbours to see who can grow the biggest vegetable or flower. Pumpkins and sunflowers are good for this.
- **START** a compost heap or bin.
- **MAKE** your own garden art. Try some clay sculpture, a papier mâché gnome, painted pebbles or mobiles made from recycled materials.
- Carry out science experiments that illustrate root growth using a bean; **SHOW** how stems work using celery; or test what seeds need to germinate and what the best conditions are for plant growth.

LEARNING AROUND
A FAIRGROUND

Whether you're visiting a large well-known fair like Nottingham's Goose Fair or London's Christmas Winter Wonderland or a smaller local fair set up in the local park, you can guarantee that the kids won't care. A fair's a fair and there's fun and learning to be had.

BEFORE YOU GO...

Fairgrounds often have a long history, traditionally providing a major source of entertainment and fun. Delve back into the beginnings of the fair you intend to visit and find out about when it first opened, what its original purpose was and who used to visit it.

If you are going to a local fair, add to the intrigue and anticipation by drawing attention to the posters and advertising surrounding the event. When is it on? Where exactly is it taking place? Based on the posters, what kind of rides and attractions do the children expect to find there?

On the actual day or night of the visit, have a talk around some of the considerations that will keep everyone safe and happy, such as: keeping valuables secure; what to do if someone gets lost; and how to make contact with each other if you get split up. There's no need to go over the top, simply remind youngsters of the basics, just for good measure.

ENCOURAGING LINES OF ENQUIRY

- How have fairgrounds changed over time? Are there any traditional influences still visible?
- Are fairground fares reasonably priced?
- Which ride or type of attraction offers the best value for money?
- How is a fairground organised – is it random or structured?
- How does the atmosphere of the fair change depending on the day of the week or the time of day?

WHILE YOU ARE THERE...

When arriving at a fairground, the temptation for children is to rush in and go on the first ride or stall they see. Instead, encourage them to walk around and take in the atmosphere and setting; they will then make better choices on how to spend their money.

ENCOURAGING DIFFERENT WAYS TO LEARN

TASTE some of the fair's fresh produce; try something traditional like candyfloss as well as something modern like chips and curry. Consider how healthy, or not the 'fayre' is. Try a local delicacy if there is one. At Nottingham's Goose Fair in England, this would be mushy peas and mint sauce.

LISTEN to the soundscape of a fairground; it's often uplifting, with many different sounds from waltzers and other attractions. Which rides are the noisiest and why? Which rides are quieter yet more atmospheric? Does the fairground noise change depending on the time of day? Is it noisier at night?

LOOK at the different shapes around the fairground. Which shape is the most common and why?

CALCULATE how much money each ride is taking. Count the number of passengers and work out how much money is being made according to the cost of the ride.

Try to **WORK OUT** the probability of winning on some of the fairground stalls.

GET PHYSICAL and feel some G-force. Modern fairgrounds often have rollercoasters, but it's the rides that rotate the riders around, often in more than one plane, that deliver the punishing G-forces and high excitement.

SUGGESTIONS

- **MAKE** a toffee apple or other fairground food such as hot dogs that you might have tried. Do the tastes stimulate memories of your experience?
- **SELL** the fair to others in the form of a poster that looks like the official fairground posters. Aim your poster at a particular audience such as one for teenagers advertising the high-thrill rides, or a poster aimed at younger children showing the stalls and smaller rides.
- **DESIGN** a new sweet or candy for a sweet-toothed friend. The new sweet can be completely original, or be a combination of elements of existing well-known sweets.
- **INVENT** new rides with different people in mind; think about your granny, a younger sibling, a white-knuckle adrenalin-addicted thrill seeker!

TIPS

- Look out for money-saving vouchers that are often printed in the local newspaper.
- Keep your costs down by taking some drinks and snacks along with you.
- Keep your valuables safe and secure.
- Car parking can be hard to find and expensive, so think about walking to the fair or using public transport.

LEARNING AROUND
AN ANIMAL SANCTUARY

Animal sanctuaries do an amazing job looking after and caring for animals in need. These sanctuaries are often run by individuals, or by small groups of people who are passionately dedicated to making a difference, even if only on a small scale.

Larger organisations often work on a grander scale and are funded as charities via grants.

Regardless of size, animal sanctuaries are virtuous in nature and very welcoming to visitors, particularly if you support their work and cause.

BEFORE YOU GO...

Preparation for your visit will vary depending on the type of sanctuary you decide to head for. A large sanctuary may cater and care for a wide range of animals; a smaller set-up might care specifically for one animal type. Look for a sanctuary that best meets your interests and those of your children. It may be as small as a local couple who run a hedgehog rescue centre, for instance. Don't let size influence your choice. Each pound or dollar or hour of voluntary work will have more impact on a smaller sanctuary.

If you are heading to a larger sanctuary, you might run the risk of totally bombarding your youngster with too much information about too many animals. To avoid this, task the kids with finding out as much as they can about about a specific animal; it will help make the whole experience more rewarding and fulfilling.

Sanctuaries are usually dynamic and entrepreneurial places, ever on the look out to increase their reach, particularly if it will help boost their coffers. The result is an events list designed to attract visitors and for you to take advantage of.

ENCOURAGING LINES OF ENQUIRY
- What are the overall aims of the sanctuary?
- Why was the sanctuary set up and how and when did it happen?
- Explore the costs of running a sanctuary.
- How many countries or continents are represented by the animals at the sanctuary?

WHILE YOU ARE THERE...

It's been hinted at already, but attending demonstrations and talks given by the experts is invaluable. Not only do they help clarify and consolidate the learning, they also help to punctuate the day and add variety to the overall experience.

On a similar note, encourage the children to talk to the staff and volunteers as sources of inspiration, facts and passion.

ENCOURAGING DIFFERENT WAYS TO LEARN

TOUCH and **HANDLE** Animal handling is often offered at sanctuaries as it's the best way to engage visitors and get their support. Whether it's a sea-life sanctuary offering a touch pool or a dog rescue centre, get hands-on.

DRAW/SKETCH animals, their expressions and behaviour; it's a great way to learn about animals because you have to watch them closely when you draw.

PHOTOGRAPH an animal's-eye-view without putting yourself at risk, of course, by taking a photo from the animal's perspective. You might be surprised what the world looks like from their viewpoint.

COLLECT as many animal names as you can, especially their Latin names.

FIND your relative by simply 'meeting' every animal in the sanctuary to read/ask/find out which animal is closest to humans in the evolutionary trail.

ASK about the animal's diet and find out what they are fed and why. For example, which food gives which nutrient/vitamin? How close is this diet to the animal's natural food source?

SUGGESTIONS

- **START** a campaign by creating a petition to bring about change that would benefit the animals in the sanctuary. Then ask family, friends and local people to support your campaign. If you feel confident enough to submit it to a local government representative, then go for it.
- **BE ENTERPRISING** by raising some money for the sanctuary. You could do a bake sale or a toy sale – it doesn't matter which. Just make sure your parent is aware of your efforts and is supportive.
- **MAKE** a wordsearch of the animal names you wrote down during your visit and send it to the centre to offer as an activity for young visitors.

TIPS

- If you have to go to the shop, encourage spending money that best supports the sanctuary, or make a donation instead.
- On arrival, get hold of a talk schedule and attend any that sound interesting.
- Be prepared for tears and emotion – and for pleas to adopt every animal you see.

LEARNING AROUND
A SPORTS GROUND

Whether you and your children are sports fans or not, a visit to a sports ground to see a professional or semi-professional game is an exciting and exhilarating experience. Certain sports matches, and the clientele they attract, are more family-friendly than others though, so select your event carefully.

BEFORE YOU GO...

Most outdoor sports are seasonal, so the choice you have will vary according to the time of year. Don't only look for the traditional sports like soccer, baseball or rugby, but consider a trip to other smaller audience sports like hockey and athletics or even niche motor sports like motocross or hot rod car racing.

Look online or in local newspapers or tourist information centres for details on when your chosen sporting occasion is to be held. You may have to book tickets ahead of the day to ensure you get seats.

A little pep talk might be needed to warn your youngsters of a few things to expect, such as large crowds, unruly elements and some basic dos and don'ts.

If your children are relatively old and hardy, you could consider travelling to the venue on public transport as this will save money and hassles with parking, and add to the atmosphere and experience of the visit.

ENCOURAGING LINES OF ENQUIRY

- What is the demographic of the spectators? Has the sport always had the same demographic? If not, why not?
- What is the total cost of the visit, taking into account travel and refreshments?
- How have sponsorship and advertising filtered into the game and the experience of it for the spectators?
- How many of the players are local talent?

WHILE YOU ARE THERE...

The thought of losing a child in a crowd is a parent's worst nightmare. Sports grounds are geared up for this, but make sure your children know where to go and what to do if they get lost. A bracelet with your phone number is a good idea that's worth considering.

ENCOURAGING DIFFERENT WAYS TO LEARN

BE the extra official by getting involved with the timekeeping, scoring or recording of player's names where appropriate. Referees usually have a notebook with them so make sure you do too. Cricket or tennis are particularly interesting games in which to try and keep score.

LISTEN to the crowd. What accents can you hear and what does this tell you about the fan base?

READ the match day programme and roughly estimate the percentages for the different content types: advertisements, photographs, reports, sponsors or news. Choose one of the articles in the programme, pretend you are the editor and read it carefully, checking for errors, spelling mistakes, incorrect grammar and punctuation. You might be surprised how many there are.

WRITE down the names of the players of the team you have gone to watch. How many of them are local names? How many of the players are from overseas? What are the effects of a club having overseas players, good and bad?

EVALUATE the players as they perform and try to identify the 'best' player. Then write down what their attributes are – fast, well-balanced movements or a good team player. During breaks, list attributes to develop in yourself.

SUGGESTIONS

- **DESIGN** a new kit for the team you have been to watch. Think of the club's historic colours and any significant patterns.
- **RATE** your experience according to your own criteria, which might include: view, comfort or excitement. Use the same criteria if you ever watch another sport.
- **THINK** critically and creatively about your experience at the ground and list between one and five changes that you think would lead to a better supporter experience. If feasible, you could write to the club and suggest them.

TIPS

- Spend five minutes orientating your child.
- Keep little ones close by, particularly when it is very busy.
- Save money by taking your own food in with you to the venue.
- Buy a programme by which you can remember the visit.

LEARNING AROUND
A HOLIDAY RESORT

A holiday resort is a place where people go for relaxation and recreation. Resorts in towns or cities are commercial venues that cater for tourists wishing to explore the area. While it may be a time to unwind and switch off from the daily routines, a holiday also provides plenty of new learning opportunities. Whether travelling abroad or within your own country, a holiday resort will trigger questions about language, culture and history, particularly if these are noticeably different from your own.

So don't switch off completely when you're away from home, but get out and about so you can explore and learn about the place you've chosen to visit.

BEFORE YOU GO...

There will be some obvious preparation associated with going away, such as packing all the gear for your family trip, but it is also good to have an informed idea of where you're going before you get there. Get the whole family involved in finding out about the holiday resort before you go. Ask each person to find out specific information about the weather for the time of year, the surrounding landscape, language spoken and any important places worthy of a visit. Have a family discussion about what you discovered and then draw up a collective list of things you want to do, places you want to see and questions you want answered when visiting.

If the holiday resort is abroad, learn a few phrases in the native language or dialect. Locals appreciate it if you can make some effort to communicate a little in their language. There are books, CDs and websites that provide key phrases, often with audio files to help you. Choose a few phrases that will be most useful and practise them before you go.

Speak to people who have been to the same holiday resort and tap into their experience. Ask them to suggest places that you must visit and activities that you should try, then add them to your own list. A conversation with them will be extremely beneficial because they will be able to enthuse and inform you about where you're going, adding to the anticipation.

ENCOURAGING LINES OF ENQUIRY
- What is the impact and effect of tourism on the local community?
- What is the resort like at low season?
- How does the resort cater for tourists from different countries?
- How has the resort changed over the last few years?

TIPS

- Take a camera and record as much as possible.
- Take along a phrase book to help you overcome any language barrier. Alternatively, jot down a few phrases before you go, to take along with you.

WHILE YOU ARE THERE...

Going on holiday broadens the horizons. Travelling to unfamiliar places and immersing yourself in a different culture can be a rich experience. It is important to travel and while there explore and appreciate the environment in order to create your own perception of the world.

ENCOURAGING DIFFERENT WAYS TO LEARN

SPEAK to someone using some of the phrases that you've learnt. Some handy phrases to use might include: hello, thank you, goodbye, yes and no.

FIND out about a trip offered to a local attraction by the hotel or tour operator and compare with the cost of doing it for yourself.

SPOT some local wildlife and photograph it. Try to find an unusual bird, animal or plant that can only be found in the area.

RECORD a short video documentary illustrating an interesting point about your holiday destination. Do some research in advance.

Go on a tour of a local attraction and **LISTEN** to a guide explain about a point of interest. Be prepared to ask lots of questions, too.

Work out the exchange rate. **FIND OUT** the cost of something and work out how much it would be in your own currency.

ODD ONE OUT – FIND THE FAKE FACT!

✗ The Eiffel Tower is modelled on the Blackpool Tower in the popular holiday resort of Blackpool in Lancashire, England.

• Benidorm is Europe and Spain's largest holiday resort, attracting five million tourists a year.

• Skegness holiday resort on the east coast of England was the location for the first Butlin's holiday resort in 1936.

• The highest ski resort in the world is Chacaltaya in Bolivia. It's so high that many of its visitors suffer altitude sickness.

BE BOLD

Try a local delicacy. Ask locals what the town or area is known for and find out where it is available. Go and visit a shop, café or restaurant where they offer the local delicacy and try some. For added boldness, ask about how they make the delicacy; you might then be able to make your own on your return home.

WHEN YOU GET BACK...

Unpacking the bags may signify the end of a trip away but hopefully the holiday will have sparked an interest that might lead to more learning opportunities.

SUGGESTIONS

• Try to **MAKE** the local delicacy that you tried – if you can. Get your friends and family members to taste some when it's ready.

• **WRITE** a description of the wildlife that you spotted. Describe what they looked like, what they ate and where they lived. If you took a photo you could add this to your facts.

• **CREATE** a Top Tips for other families. What would you have liked to know before going? Think about your Top Tips that will help others.

TRAVEL AND TRANSPORT

LEARNING AROUND
A TRAIN STATION

A fascination for trains is deeply rooted in our history and culture due to the impact that the modern railway industry has had on the movement of people and goods over distances great and small. Early stationary steam engines were used to facilitate the mining industry and then, in the early 1800s, the steam locomotive was developed as industry and human expansion was revolutionised. The rest as they say, is history.

Train stations, or stops, enable people and freight to be loaded and unloaded, and offer connections between lines and other modes of transport, such as buses. They are therefore critical to the functioning of an effective rail service.

BEFORE YOU GO...

There are different ways to explore trains and train stations. Here are some ideas:

1. Visit your local mainline station. Find your nearest station and get to know it.

2. Travel between stations. Go on a journey, getting to know a series of stations.

3. Visit a well-known station in a major city or capital city.

4. Go to a station that runs part-time; it is likely to be centered on the running of a steam train line.

5. Visit a living museum and learn about stations and trains in an historical context.

6. Attend a 'special event' day.

The kind of visit you choose will depend on the learning focus you have in mind. For example, if you want your child to understand how trains and stations facilitate the movement of people, then ideas one to three might be best for that.

Whereas a more historical perspective will be best catered for by ideas four to six, where trains of a bygone age are kept maintained and running part-time by teams of dedicated enthusiasts.

If you are short of time or don't think a visit to a train station warrants all of your spare time, then tie this learning into a train journey you might need to take at some point. With a little bit of preparation, you will be able to turn an everyday train journey into a valuable learning experience as well as having activities to keep the kids busy on the journey. All aboard!

ENCOURAGING LINES OF ENQUIRY
- What are the features of a train station?
- What services and facilities do train stations offer? Is it the same for all stations?
- How well connected is the station?
- What goods traffic and passenger traffic travel through the station?
- How do side-track stations differ to terminus stations?

TIPS
- If you can, take the young ones on a selection of trains: high speed, steam or regular diesel 'chuggers'.
- Special event days such as Thomas the Tank Engine or World War Two commemorations are entertaining, immersive, a great day out for all.
- Show interest in the tasks and this will rub off on your learners.
- Collect some timetables for follow-up work.

WHILE YOU ARE THERE...

Try and take in as much of the station as you can. Encourage children to look beyond the trains themselves and to look for old signs, carvings and commemorative plaques. The key to understanding the importance of trains and connectivity is to people-watch.

ENCOURAGING DIFFERENT WAYS TO LEARN

LOOK and **LISTEN**. People-watching involves sitting and observing their movements and behaviours. Train stations are a great place to do this because they tend to be busy with people and activity each and every day. Behaviour patterns will vary according to the time of day and the time of year. Make some observations and identify a pattern. During off-peak periods, for instance, passengers are often more relaxed.

GAUGE how busy a train station is by simply trying to walk from one end of it to the other in a straight line. You'll be amazed at how much zig-zagging you have to do during busy periods.

CATEGORISE the kinds of shops there are at the station. Try and explain why such shops are present at the station in terms of the human movements and needs.

MAKE rubbings of any plaques or etchings around the station that can give an indication of its age.

CALCULATE how punctual the trains are by selecting a sample of trains (for example, all the trains that leave from platform 1 in an hour) and recording if they leave on time or not. At the end of the time period, find the total number of minutes delay and divide it by the number of trains you recorded.

ODD ONE OUT – FIND THE FAKE FACT!
- Baker Street Station in London was the world's first station to be completely underground.
- Grand Central Terminal in New York has 44 platforms and 67 tracks.
- ✗ The first ever railway station was in England.
- Shinjuku Station in Tokyo, Japan, is the world's busiest station in terms of passengers by day who use it.

BE BOLD
Security in busy stations has been stepped up over recent years. Ask a station security guard or a transport police man/woman about their job to find out what it is they are on the lookout for.

WHEN YOU GET BACK...

Railways are one of the most environmentally friendly ways to travel, but there are factors that can discourage people from using trains, such as cost, reliability, comfort and safety. Discuss with your child what changes could be made to encourage more people to use the railways. See if, as a family, you can feasibly use more public transport than you currently do.

SUGGESTIONS
- Using the timetables you collected, PLAN a multi-stop journey from place A to B that involves train changes. Compare the time of that journey with the time estimation for the same journey A to B using a car. Repeat for a different journey. Deduce whether train travel is more efficient or not.
- Find and READ Robert Louis Stevenson's poem *From a Railway Carriage*, and consider how relevant it is to modern train travel. Write a modern version of the poem using sounds and sights from journeys you have made.

LEARNING AROUND
A FERRY

A trip on a ferry, regardless of size, evokes a sense of excitement, exploration and possibly even new horizons. Adventure, islands containing treasure or even stories of pirates might capture your imagination. Or maybe it's the science behind flotation that grabs your attention. Whatever floats your boat, make your next ferry trip one to remember.

BEFORE YOU GO...

Before your trip, make sure you all know about the route the boat will be taking, and where you will end up. It might be a day trip or an overnight ocean crossing – it doesn't matter. What are the departure and destination points? What is the duration of the trip? What is the body of water you are crossing called? Share and answer these questions together.

A trip over water offers an opportunity to learn about this amazing habitat. Look for leaflets on sea life, seabirds and other interesting things to look for. This will make the trip memorable and educational.

Oh, and lastly, be prepared! Make sure you have clothing to protect you and keep you dry and warm when out on deck. After all, the experience will not be as exciting if your young crew do not spend a good part of it out on deck in the fresh air!

ENCOURAGING LINES OF ENQUIRY

- How is the boat designed to keep passengers safe when at sea/out on the water?
- Boats are just forms of human transport. Where are the passengers from and where are they going?
- What evidence is there out at sea of the negative human impact on our oceans?

WHILE YOU ARE THERE...

Boats are not really places for children to roam around unsupervised. A rough sea can throw even a car ferry around and a light swell can make a small day boat bob around like a cork. The risk of falling overboard is a real one, so keep your crew supervised accordingly.

ENCOURAGING DIFFERENT WAYS TO LEARN

LOOK at the boat from the outside before you board it. Look at how much of it is above and below the water. See how the bow (front) is shaped and compare it to the stern (back). Can you explain why this is?

EXPLORE how child-friendly your ferry is by exploring as much of it as you can, and by mapping or logging what each area is used for, including food and refreshments, a bar for adults, seating or a children's play area. Colour the map with each area to show how much or how little the ferry caters for young people.

GET ACTIVE with a game. Start at one of the boat's muster stations and split into teams of two. While one of the teams stay at the muster station, the other goes for a wander around the boat. After an agreed time, say 10 minutes, the team at the muster station phones the other teams. They have to get back to the muster point as quickly as they can.

SENSORY Get someone to take a photo of one of the ship's signs on their phone, then see if you can find where the photo was taken. Then swap roles and repeat.

SUGGESTIONS
- Get a toy boat and try to load it with as much weight as you can. **EXPERIMENT** with small objects or a single, large one. See which method of loading is the most effective.
- **MAKE** a boat and see if it floats, or **DESIGN** a boat in a 3D program like Google SketchUp or Minecraft.
- **WRITE** a short story based around a boat trip. It could be about a stowaway, a wreck or a journey. It could be original or based on a children's story.

TIPS
To make sure your children are happy and ship-shape, try to ensure they don't get travel sickness by:
- Taking travel bands with you.
- Keeping the horizon in view.
- Staying near the centre of the boat, where the pitch and roll are minimised.

LEARNING AROUND
AN AIRPORT

There is something so intriguing and fascinating about airports, not only in a sort of geeky plane-spotting way, but also in an amazing and awesome kind of way. Seeing a huge object over 300 metric tonnes in weight – more than a couple of overweight blue whales – coming in to land seems to defy the laws of gravity. Watching the approach path of a busy airport, and seeing planes land and take off every three minutes or so, demonstrates human ingenuity at its best. Harness this awesomeness, and see your children's learning run away.

BEFORE YOU GO...

If you don't live near an airport then you'll need to have a look on a map to find one that you can vist. Do some initial research into not only the location, but also which airport has the best outdoor viewpoints and indoor viewing gallery. The main thrill for a child will be to get as close as possible to the planes that land and take off, so make sure there are plenty of opportunities for this.

At some airports it is possible to get close to the runway, while still staying safely on the outside of the perimeter fence. This makes it possible to watch in wonder as the planes almost drop out of the sky right above your head. Take a picnic to munch on in between incoming planes, then relax and enjoy the show with your chicken wings and plane crisps.

Exciting learning can take place all round an airport and as part of travels or during a discreet visit on a wet weekend when there isn't much else to do. Get your picnic ready, pack your day bag and make your way towards the terminal for boarding. Your learning is ready for departure – enjoy the EdVenture!

ENCOURAGING LINES OF ENQUIRY
- What does the airport look like from above?
- Which airlines use the airport, and which countries do they fly to?
- What are the steps you go through between arriving at the airport and boarding a plane?
- Is air travel bad for the environment?

WHILE YOU ARE THERE...

Airports can be very busy and stressful places, and not ideal for letting children loose to explore and investigate. You will need to supervise your child during any activities inside the airport building, so make them aware of the type of environment they are in and what is and isn't acceptable. Outside of the airport is better for children and offers the best way to get them close to aeroplanes that are flying.

ENCOURAGING DIFFERENT WAYS TO LEARN

LISTEN The noise of an aeroplane is an exciting stimulus to explore. Depending on which way the planes are landing/taking off, according to the wind direction, one end of the runway will have planes landing, the other planes taking off. The noise a plane produces varies significantly depending on what the engines are doing.

Inside the airport, focus on the different announcements that are made and try to categorise them: security announcements, passenger information or staff notices. What is the balance of the messages and why?

LOOK carefully at the colours and designs on the planes at the airport. Encourage children to try and decipher the tail designs and explain why certain objects or symbols are used.

When **OUT AND ABOUT**, if possible, speak to people inside the airport and around in the local area to find out their opinions on the airport. Do people using the airport have different views to people living close to it?

SUGGESTIONS

- **DEBATE** with someone as to whether airports are a good thing or a bad thing. Remember to support and justify the points made by providing examples.
- **MAKE** an air-propelled toy by attaching a balloon onto it then partly blowing up the balloon and releasing it.
- **DESIGN** a logo for your own airline. What would be on it and why?
- **IMAGINE** you were opening a new shop for the terminal building. What would you sell? Make a poster to advertise it.
- **INVESTIGATE** if it is cheaper per mile to travel by car, bus, train or aeroplane.

TIPS

- Airports are very cosmopolitan places and therefore offer children a good location for getting a real sense of how diverse the world is.
- Use Google Maps to get a sense of scale of an airport.
- Consider the pros and cons of living next to an airport.
- Do a cost comparison between an airport shop and a high street store to help children determine and explain the airport 'mark-up'.

LEARNING AROUND
A BOAT RIDE

Travelling anywhere by boat is an exciting and memorable event. It doesn't matter if the ride is a short chug down a canal or river on a cruiser, or a three-hour ride over sea swell on a wildlife-spotting boat trip. Boat rides usually incur a cost, so make an informed selection about a ride that offers both good value and a good experience.

BEFORE YOU GO...

Have a family get-together to discuss the trip and decide what you might need to take with you: binoculars, picnic, swimming costumes and towel, for instance. This will depend on the trip and the time of year, but thinking things through will help you get the most out of the trip and avoid any regrets about items you've forgotten to bring. It's also worth ringing the boat trip provider ahead of the journey to see if they recommend anything specific that you should take. They will also be able to advise on the practicalities of clothing and how best to protect yourselves from the elements.

If you plan to hire your own boat, it's a good idea to familiarise yourself with the layout of the waterway you will be boating on. You will be given an introduction by the hire company, but take a look at the area, key place names and milestones to head for on Google Maps, as this will do you no harm. You can also plan your route, stop-off points and what you are going to do where.

ENCOURAGING LINES OF ENQUIRY
- Where are you going? How long will it take to get there? How fast will you be travelling?
- Are there any rules and regulations that the boat operators have to abide by? Why are there such rules and regulations?
- How is the movement of a boat different to that of a car? Include steering, turning and stopping.
- How might boats and boat trips impact on the environment and wildlife?

WHILE YOU ARE THERE...

It's likely that your child will be excited about being in a boat – and rightly so. Let them express this excitement and don't stifle it. If you can, let young ones have a go at the helm to experience how the boat moves and steers.

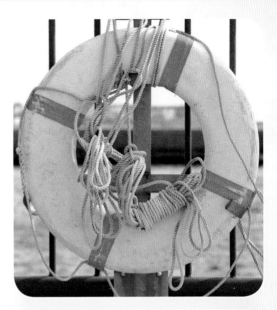

ENCOURAGING DIFFERENT WAYS TO LEARN

LISTEN to the sounds of the waterway or ocean – such sounds are considered calming and relaxing. Tune into people's conversations and moods to see if this is true in reality.

TALK to the crew members, including the skipper (or captain) to find out what it is like working on the boat or at the hire company. What do they like about the job, and what do they dislike?

GET ACTIVE when at locks or mooring up. Ask to help with the jobs that need doing and really understand what it's like to be in charge of a boat.

You have to **GET WET** when there's water all around you. Go for a paddle if you stop anywhere on the trip.

PHOTOGRAPH or **SKETCH** the different parts of the boat, and learn associated and useful vocabulary such as: stern, bow, port, starboard, tiller, rudder and mast.

SUGGESTIONS
- **PLAY** with your toy boats in the bath – even relive the trip you had. It doesn't matter what your age is, you're never too old!
- **WRITE** a letter to the boat hire company or trip provider to say thank you and to explain what you learned/found out during the trip.
- **DESIGN** a leaflet on a computer to promote the boat trip or hire company you used. Add the photographs you took and include any information or facts that you learned.

TIPS
- Keep children's arms and fingers inside the boat when alongside a bank, jetty or other boats.
- Take extra clothing, especially if venturing out offshore.
- Make sure buoyancy aids are always worn.

LEARNING AROUND
A BRIDGE

Famous bridges like the Golden Gate Bridge, Tower Bridge and Sydney's Harbour Bridge are global icons, tourist attractions visited by millions of people every year. Part of the attraction is the scale and design of them, another is the sense of fascination and pride at the human ingenuity involved in creating such a construction.

On the other hand, a span bridged by beams of wood or stone and even a fallen tree qualify as bridges on equal merit, as they perform the same function as some of the iconic greats.

We all tend to take bridges for granted as we use them every day without noticing them.

BEFORE YOU GO...

With all this in mind, it's worth trying to give your child the complete bridge experience. Children will enjoy visiting and crossing impressive bridges and marvelling at their scale, but will learn as much, if not more, about aspects of bridge construction if they get hands-on and build one of their own.

Try to find examples of different bridges in your local area, or somewhere on holiday. Look at the different construction techniques used: beam, truss, cantilever, arch, tied arch, suspension and cable-stayed bridges. Look at examples on the internet, too, and try to classify some of the world's iconic bridges into the main construction categories. Depending on the age and stage of your child, apply some understanding of the science of forces in bridge design. The forces that all bridges have to overcome are, in differing degrees: compression, tension, shearing, bending and twisting (or torsion).

To help a child develop their analytical and enquiry skills, it's important to encourage them to think of the purpose of the things around them, such as the implementation of science and engineering in bridge building. Why do humans go to great lengths to build complex, and often expensive, bridge structures? While the engineering and science is complex, the answer is surprisingly straightforward: to make journeys quicker and more direct. In simple terms, to make shortcuts.

If ever we needed an example to demonstrate the insatiable desire of humans to make life easier, quicker and more instant, then bridge building is one of our great inventions.

ENCOURAGING LINES OF ENQUIRY

- What are the facts – span, construction, height, weight?
- How does the building of the bridge impact on journey times and distance?
- How well used is the bridge?
- What are the factors that make bridges expensive to build and maintain?

TIPS
- Familiarise yourself with bridge types and their terminology.
- Visit a range of bridges if you can.
- Bridges and traffic go together, so beware.

WHILE YOU ARE THERE...

Enjoy the thrill of walking across a large-scale bridge such as a suspension bridge. Look up the concrete towers and ponder the effort and skill required to build such a structure. Ensure that children come away in awe and respect of this feat of human ingenuity.

ENCOURAGING DIFFERENT WAYS TO LEARN

Simply **WALK** across the bridge and back to grasp its span and scale. This is a must-do task.

OBSERVE the traffic using the bridge by carrying out a simple survey of vehicles, people and bikes. Carry out the same survey at a different time of day to determine patterns in traffic flow. Then try and explain the patterns you have identified.

CALCULATE how much the bridge might make if it were to become a toll bridge (if it isn't already). Make a calculation based on traffic flow in 10, 15, 30 or 60 minutes to calculate how much money is taken in an hour. Use this figure to calculate revenue per day, per week, per month and per year. If you can, find out how much the bridge costs in maintenance overheads to see if the numbers tally.

IDENTIFY the features of the bridge construction from earlier preparation work. Take photos and use them when you get home to write a pseudo-engineering report.

Use a smartphone audio looping app to collect sounds such as cars passing, footsteps, tapping the barriers – any sound that can be made on the bridge. **CREATE** a soundscape for the particular bridge you have visited. Compare it to the soundscape of a different bridge.

LOOK for shapes in the bridge's structure: triangles, circles, rectangles, arches etc. What does this tell you about the inherent strengths of different shapes?

ODD ONE OUT – FIND THE FAKE FACT!

- The oldest standing bridge is in China.
- ✗ Iron replaced steel in bridge design because it has a higher tensile strength.
- In suspension bridges, the roadway is literally hanging on long cables.
- The height of Sydney Harbour Bridge changes as the metal contracts and expands in the heat.

BE BOLD

Phone up the bridge operator to find out about the maintenance and associated costs required to keep the bridge functional. Ask if you can be given a guided tour around the bridge.

THE CONSTRUCTION OF A SUSPENSION BRIDGE

Compression

Tension   Tension

Main suspension cable

Deck

Suspender cables

Tower

Weight

Compression

Anchorage block

Tower foundation

WHEN YOU GET BACK...

To reinforce the ubiquitous nature of bridges, play 'spot the bridge' when you are on the way home in the car, bus or train. It is a simple game that involves shouting out the name of the type of bridge construction used for each bridge that you see or are travelling over or under. The first person to correctly shout out the construction, e.g. 'arch!' or 'truss', gets a point.

SUGGESTIONS

- MAKE a bridge out of a construction kit or thin pieces of modelling wood and a glue gun. Use your knowledge of structures and shapes to make the strongest bridge you can. Test the bridge using weights.
- MAKE a simple Top Trump fact card for the bridge, including a photo or sketch. Make other cards for other bridges around the world.
- LOOK for a short span in your garden or nearby ditch and use natural materials to bridge the gap.

BY THE
WATER

LEARNING AROUND
A BEACH

If you've been on holiday to a coastal resort then life will literally have been a beach! Children love them and so they should, as there is a wealth of fun and learning to be had, both in and out of the water.

Should you live somewhere like the UK then you are lucky enough to never be very far away from a coastline and therefore a beach. If you live a long way from the seaside, beaches can still be found on lakes and near river systems, so don't despair.

BEFORE YOU GO...

A lot of learning can take place before you head out to the beach, learning that will be really useful for the enriching experience that you can have when you do arrive.

Children will know that the sea comes in and it goes out but they may not be aware of the concept of tides. Tides are fascinating from a science perspective as well as from a human viewpoint. They dictate when fishing boats can come and go from ports, when lobster nets can be collected and when deciding the best time to head to the beach to picnic, bodyboard, walk the dog or to surf.

Coupled with the science learning behind tides – how they are affected by the gravitational inter-relationship between the Earth, Sun and Moon – is the concept of a tidal timetable: accurate times for high and low tides, calculated well in advance. Not only is it fascinating to find out how tides work and timetables can be predicted, but also it has safety implications. Knowing the time of high tide might prevent you being 'cut off' by an incoming tide. Make sure all

family members are aware of the tide times for the beach you are visiting, before you get there.

Similarly, if you plan to let the children into the sea, make them aware of the conventions used by the lifeguards that will be monitoring the coast. Family-friendly beaches will use the internationally recognised system of flags to notify the status of the water, whether it is safe to swim in and whether lifeguards are on duty, for example. Chat about this before you head to the beach and collectively refresh and familiarise yourselves using the information boards positioned on the beachfront you visit.

ENCOURAGING LINES OF ENQUIRY

- Why is the beach resort you have visited so popular?
- Which are the most popular areas of the beach, and why?
- How do the ocean and its tides affect the beach?
- How and why is the beach important to the tourism industry?

TIPS

- Learn about the different flag systems that lifeguards use.
- Learn about currents, including safety tips.
- Learn about local sea life, including dangers such as weever fish, sharks or jellyfish.
- Look around the seaside town near the beach and count how many ice-cream shops there are.

WHILE YOU ARE THERE...

The learning opportunities that present themselves at a beach will vary to a large degree on the particular beach you visit, so keep on the lookout for things like rock pools or groynes and sea walls, as well as the patterns of activity of the tourists who are wandering around.

ENCOURAGING DIFFERENT WAYS TO LEARN

FEEL the beach by having a touchy-feely sensory quiz. Give the kids a bag each so they can head out and collect 'samples' from the beach environment. Get them to look for seaweed, rocks, stones and seashells. Then, each family member feels the items in the bag, without looking of course, and has to guess what they think they are.

GET PHYSICAL and try to stop the sea. There is no better way to demonstrate the relentlessness and power of the ocean than to try and stop it by building a wall or sea defence. See how long you can prevent its advance, but be warned your efforts will be fruitless.

THINK about how destructive the sea can be and use this as a stimulus to learn about the traditional methods and modern engineering solutions that humans have tried, and continue to use, to protect our beaches and preserve our coastal towns.

VISUALISE the problem of litter pollution by spending just a short amount of time collecting non-biodegradable items left on beaches as a result of littering, on land and at sea. Make sure the kids are supervised and use a litter picker.

BE BOLD
Make a stand against litterers and irresponsible dog owners – challenge people that drop litter or don't pick up dog waste.

WHEN YOU GET BACK...

Your enjoyment and learning at the beach doesn't need to stop when you get home, particularly if you have brought home the plastic litter you collected during your beach clean-up (see suggestions).

Similarly, an exciting experience at a rock pool might stimulate some research work at home on marine life.

SUGGESTIONS
- **LEARN** about lighthouse signals, and explain why each lighthouse has a unique number and rate of flashes.
- **SPOT** stars by visiting the beach after dark. The lack of light pollution means beaches have some of the best 'dark night skies'.
- **PLAY** traditional beach games such as volleyball, rounders, boules or kite flying at your local park.
- **MAKE** a plastic sculpture from your beach waste to highlight the issue of plastic pollution and its impact on oceans and wildlife.

LEARNING AROUND
A CLIFF

Cliffs occur not only at coastal areas, but are also commonly found in mountainous regions as well as along rivers. Composed of steep faces made of erosion-resistant material like sedimentary or igneous rocks, cliffs often contribute to a dramatic and imposing landscape and are always interesting geographical features to explore.

BEFORE YOU GO...

A bit of background reading into basic geology, covering rock types and the processes of weathering and erosion will give you the confidence to accurately describe and explain some of the things you may see or find when you arrive at your chosen cliff venue.

Think about your child's interests to see if there might be an opportunity to tap into them on this kind of visit. A child with an interest in fossils and dinosaurs, for example, will relish the opportunity to go to a fossil-rich coastline or river cliff. Similarly, a child interested in ornithology will see great appeal in visiting a cliff that is home to nesting seabirds such as the puffin. A more active child will see excitement in a cliff visit if there are opportunities to rock climb or coasteer.

Like most things, if you present an idea to your child in the right way to make it appealing and worth their while, then you'll have no problem with motivating them to join you.

ENCOURAGING LINES OF ENQUIRY
- What are the physical characteristics of the cliff area you are visiting? Look at height, age, and rock type.
- What processes formed, and continue to form, the cliff?
- What would the area have looked like 1000 years ago? A million years ago? Why?
- How do humans interact with the cliff, if at all?

WHILE YOU ARE THERE...

Without wishing to go over-the-top on safety, cliffs do present real dangers. There is the possibility of falling from the top or of being injured by falling rocks when at the bottom. So keep little ones close at hand and if the cliffs look unstable from below, they probably are.

ENCOURAGING DIFFERENT WAYS TO LEARN

PATIENCE and **PERSEVERANCE** are valuable qualities to possess (especially in today's must-have-it-now culture) and can be harnessed through activities like shell collecting and fossil hunting. Encourage your children to keep looking and not to give in. Praise the effort that they are putting in to the process of finding a shell or fossil, rather than concentrating on the nature of what they are finding.

Promote the importance of **TALKING** and **LISTENING** by encouraging your children to seek the knowledge of experts. Get them to take any fossils that they find into a local gem shop or museum so they can have them identified locally.

For more **ACTIVE** kids, take them coasteering (climbing along the cliffs and jumping into the sea). This is definitely not 'tombstoning' and is definitely not something you should embark on alone. Instead, use a local adventure provider. The same goes for climbing; use a provider that has the local knowledge of where and where not to go.

Get **TOUCHY-FEELY** with the cliff bottom. All this means is to pick up different pebbles and stones and bits of fallen cliff rock. Try and identify the rock or stone type through touch.

SUGGESTIONS
- **EXHIBIT** any rocks, pebbles and fossils found at the cliff. Label them as if they were for display in a museum.
- **BAKE** some chocolate crispy cakes, experimenting with different types and amounts of chocolate binding. When they have cooled, rub two of the crispy cakes together to see which one breaks and crumbles the most, or the first. This might help you explain the process of erosion.
- **LOOK** for suitable recipes online.

TIPS
- Cliffs are inherently dangerous so make sure everyone is aware of the dangers.
- If you going fossil hunting you will need some tools: a small pick, a rock hammer or even just a kitchen knife to help prise out your finds.

LEARNING AROUND
A RIVER

Rivers form a key part of the water cycle, forming an arterial network to take rainwater downhill and back to the oceans, providing us with fresh water for drinking and for industry.

Rivers can flow overground or underground and are responsible for erosion and abrasion and the creation of impressive cave systems and river valleys. They are also important ecosystems for wildlife, ranging from microscopic to huge.

Many of the world's major cities are located on or close to a river as they are important for the transportation of goods and people, fulfilling a significant function.

BEFORE YOU GO...

In schools, children learn about the water cycle (or hydrological cycle) from a young age, and in so doing learn some of the key vocabulary associated with rivers. Generally, using the correct technical language is useful as it helps you to speak more accurately about the relevant topic, and the same applies with rivers. So, refresh everyone's understanding of terms of features of a river system, such as:

Meander, tributary, trunk, source, branch, rapids, mouth, estuary, bank, bed, alluvial, effluent, sediment, silt, watershed, channel, oxbow lake.

It is important to choose the river you are to visit with your particular aims in mind. For example, if you want to study how a river is used for freight transportation, you might be best visiting an estuary, as this is often where docks are situated. Alternatively, if you want to study some of the geography of a river – the features, flow and depth – then a location further upriver would be better. Maps and websites are good sources of inspiration and time spent choosing your location before you head out will be well worth it.

Another approach might be to try and cover more than one section of the river in a day, and while you probably won't be able to trace the entire river system from source to sea, you could feasibly see a few different sections of the river by walking and driving or cycling. This will enable you to compare and contrast a narrow fast-flowing section with a wider meandering section, before heading further downriver to see the latter stages of the river before it finally meets the sea.

ENCOURAGING LINES OF ENQUIRY
- What makes a river flow at different speeds?
- What are the threats to river ecosystems?
- Who looks after the rivers (official and volunteers)?
- Is there evidence that the river was or still is used for transportation?

TIPS

- Get wet and enjoy the river. Go prepared to get a bit damp.
- Beware of tree swings you might find.
- Discourage jumping in unless water depth has been tested.
- Be aware of currents and flow.
- Take a measure and a timer to help with surveying work.

WHILE YOU ARE THERE...

Learning about rivers doesn't have to be heavy and formal. In fact, make the visit fun and informal to make the learning flow. Aim to make the experience interactive and immersive, literally perhaps, and ensure that it's also hands-on – and feet in!

··

ENCOURAGING DIFFERENT WAYS TO LEARN

SAMPLE the water to assess its quality. Is it clear? Is any tiny animal-life activity visible? Test the pH of the water with litmus paper.

MEASURE the speed and depth of the different river sections. Use a ping-pong ball or a small boat and time how long it takes to travel a set distance, e.g. 10 metres (yards) at a wide part. Compare the flow speed of a different section, e.g. a narrow, shallow section. Measure the depths carefully at each section. Is there a relationship between depth and flow speed?

RIDE the river on an inflatable tyre or tube. What better way to gauge the flow speed than to literally 'go with the flow'!

LISTEN to the river in different places. Get creative and think of some appropriate personifications for the river, based on its different voices, e.g. a babbling brook, a giggling stream or a vociferous waterfall.

HIKE and **CAMP** as you walk the river from source to sea, sketching and labelling as you go.

MOUNT a bridge or go up a tall building in order to get an aerial view of the river section. The higher you go, the more interesting the view, as the river's meandering route gradually becomes visible.

PLAY I-spy river creatures and river inhabitants.

Keep your **EYES** and **EARS** sharp, and keep quiet and still; your reward may be sightings of the river's shy inhabitants: kingfishers or otters.

ODD ONE OUT – FIND THE FAKE FACT!
- The Nile is the world's longest river.
- ✗ Rivers contain either fresh water or salt water.
- The Yellow River in China used to be known as the Black River.
- An oxbow lake is formed when a wide meander is 'cut off' from the main river passage.

BE BOLD
Phone the rivers agency to report any findings you make about water quality, or concerns you have about the river you have visited, or its inhabitants.

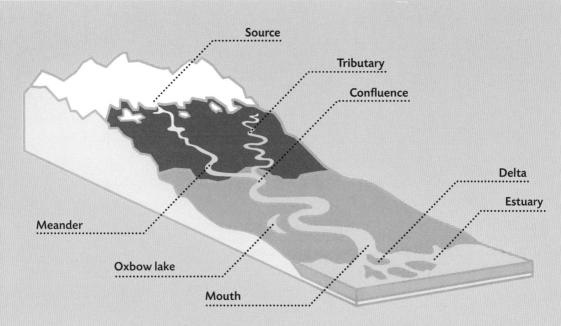

Source

Tributary

Confluence

Delta

Estuary

Meander

Oxbow lake

Mouth

RIVER TERMINOLOGY

WHEN YOU GET BACK...

Hopefully your family will return from a river visit with a greater awareness of not only the river's geographical features, but also the issues affecting the river ecosystem and its inhabitants, such as water quality and pollution. Help maintain this awareness by looking and listening out for river-related stories in the media, particularly local ones, and sharing them with your children.

SUGGESTIONS
- **INVESTIGATE** a local stream or river and give it a health check based on criteria you come up with, e.g. diversity of wildlife or visible signs of pollution. Research how rivers can be polluted and look out for the signs.
- **LOOK** on Google Maps for extreme river features – oxbow lakes, deltas and impressive meanders, rapid sections and waterfalls.
- **LOOK** for websites that allow you to monitor river levels and animal activity from a distance. Some rivers have webcams that allow you to watch for salmon returning to their spawning grounds.

LEARNING AROUND
A LAKE

For the purposes of this activity, we can define a lake by talking about largish areas of water that are surrounded by land. Depending on where you live, a lake might be known as a pool, a lagoon, a tarn, a loch or another such name. This project aims to help you get the most out of a visit to one of those places.

BEFORE YOU GO...

If you have a focus to your visit, the chances are you will get more out of it. We'll take it as read that one of the purposes is to have a fun time there together, but going with one or two more specific ideas is also a good idea. Maybe it's the summer and you want to go for a wild swim? Maybe there are migrating birds gathering. Maybe you want to go pond dipping?

Defining your focus beforehand will identify any preparation or kit items you might need, including a fishing net, water tray and magnifying glass for pond dipping. It may also help you to decide when to go. If you wish to see frogs returning to a pond to lay eggs, then you'll know to head down to the lake in early spring (in the UK at least).

You may also want to time your visit to coincide with an organised event such as a guided walk or a 'meet the ranger' day.

ENCOURAGING LINES OF ENQUIRY
- What are the main uses of the lake?
- What makes a lake? What are its features and inhabitants?
- What impacts a lake in a good and bad way?

WHILE YOU ARE THERE...

Something that is worth looking out for in the summer holidays is a 'have a go' day at a lake that has a resident sailing club. They run these days to try and encourage people into water sports and are a great way to have a first taste of this expensive sport.

ENCOURAGING DIFFERENT WAYS TO LEARN

DIP in the lake using a fishing net to identify as many species of pond life as you can. Have a 'beauty' contest and choose your three winning beauties. How you define beautiful is up to you!

MAKE a food chain that includes some of the animals found in and around the lake. Then try to expand the food chain into a food web for the lake.

GET ACTIVE and have a go at windsurfing, sailing or stand-up paddle boarding as they can be a relaxing way to enjoy the lake from on top of the water.

TWEET and **TWITTER** to the resident birds by copying their bird calls or songs. Make sure you identify them, too. Ask a ranger or bird-spotter if you need help. If you get the pitch and pattern accurate, you may be able to have a 'conversation' with a bird.

GET CREATIVE and make up memorable names to help you recall birds by their sounds, e.g. the great tit could be called the 'bicycle pump bird'.

CHILL OUT on a hot day by sitting on the bank with your feet in the water. Close your eyes, listen carefully and drift away somewhere in your imagination. Relaxing like this is good for the mind and the soul.

SUGGESTIONS

- If you tried and enjoyed a water sport, have a look online for a club or training centre near to where you live.
- DRAW and COLOUR some of the animals and minibeasts that live in a lake (to scale if you can) and then make a food chain/web mobile with pieces of string connecting the animals in the appropriate order.
- LEARN about some of the conservation issues applicable to lakes and ponds, then visit a lake or pond near where you live to see if and how much they apply.

TIPS

- Check for signs and information to see if the lake has blue-green algae, which can be harmful to children and dogs.
- Take a change of clothes, especially if you plan to try any water-based activities.
- Take wellies or waterproof shoes.
- Take a minibeast identification sheet/app if you are going pond dipping.

LEARNING AROUND
AN ISLAND

An island is a piece or area of land that is surrounded by water. Some islands are huge, like Greenland, the biggest island in the world, while some are small, like the kind you might find in a river. As you can imagine, there are countless islands around the world and their types vary enormously. Some islands are heavily populated, while others are remote and completely uninhabited. This latter type of island often features in adventure stories and movies, because throughout history islands have been stopping-off places for ships.

BEFORE YOU GO...

With the above in mind, have a think about what kind of island it is that you are going to strike out for. This will determine everything else about your trip: how to get there, what to do there, how long to stay there. You may be venturing out one afternoon to try and reach that river island you've walked past many a time (you know, the one that usually has a heron sat on it), or heading out for an overnight sleepover on an uninhabited island off the coast of Scotland.

Google Maps is a great free tool for checking out locations and planning routes and journeys. Just 'Google Map' your destination and start by identifying the surrounding body of water and the type of terrain or landscape on the island. Use the measuring tool to work out some basics like the distance to the island, perimeter of the island and that kind of thing.

You may need to decide how you are going to get to the island. Will it be by canoe, kayak, organised boat trip, walking or swimming? If you have your own means of transport, aim to find a beach that you can only reach via the sea (again, Google Maps will help with this).

Children's adventure stories and films might be your stimulus for visiting an island. If they are, you are certainly going out with the right intentions: to have fun and adventure. Perhaps you plan to get 'unintentionally' marooned on the island with your young crew member? Now wouldn't that be exciting?

Another fun focus to have for your island trip is to look for an island with some interesting place names, e.g. Mussel Bay or Smuggler's Cove. If you find a fascinating or thought-provoking name, make that your destination.

ENCOURAGING LINES OF ENQUIRY
- Was the island once part of the mainland? Why isn't it now?
- How has the island developed/changed/modernised over the years?
- What problems does the island face today, if any?
- How might the story *Treasure Island*, or *Swallows and Amazons*, have played out on this island?

WHILE YOU ARE THERE...

When alighting onto the island, get into role from your first step onwards. Whether you are Jim Hawkins or Long John Silver from *Treasure Island*, or John, Titty or Roger from *Swallows and Amazons*, have fun playing out a favourite storyline. If this isn't your thing, just get exploring!

ENCOURAGING DIFFERENT WAYS TO LEARN

WALK the perimeter of the island or coastline.

LOOK at a map and compass to identify north, south, east and west. Identify features on the island and compare where they are in relation to each other.

MAKE a compass on the beach or somewhere else prominent using stones, rocks and driftwood so that any other 'sailors' that might visit will be able to orientate themselves.

Be a cartographer and **MAKE** an outline map of the island, then complete it with added features that you can see and find. See how well you did by checking it against a 'real' map of the island.

PLANT some treasure on 'your' island, then leave a treasure map behind to help someone find the treasure. It is a bit like leaving a geocache, but the old-fashioned way 'me hearty'!

BUILD a shelter, make a meal and, if you can, then sleep out in your shelter like Robinson Crusoe would have done.

ODD ONE OUT – FIND THE FAKE FACT!

- The Galapagos Islands are a UNESCO World Heritage Site.
- Hawaii is the only US state with a tropical rain forest.
- ✗ Madagascar is the third largest island in the world.
- Tasmania, off Australia, is the home to the Tasmanian devil.

BE BOLD

When you have hidden your treasure, challenge someone else on the island to use your treasure map to find it.
Or, go for a swim!

WHEN YOU GET BACK...

It's likely that your island trip felt like (and actually was) an adventure, something you will remember, and maybe even repeat again another time. If that is the case, then great. Remember, there are literally thousands of islands to choose from and no two islands will ever be the same so your adventure will be just as unique next time round.

SUGGESTIONS

- **PLAY** treasure island battleships. Draw grids on two copies of the map outline. Mark on five pieces of treasure and take it in turn to guess coordinates in order to find the other person's treasure.
- **MAKE** up your own treasure island instruction game to play with friends. Call out instructions like 'north' and run to one wall, 'dig for treasure' and carry out a digging action... you get the idea.
- **MAKE** an island dessert out of ice cream, biscuit and chocolate sauce. Name it after the island that you visited.
- **READ** an island adventure story – *Swallows and Amazons*, *Treasure Island* or *Lord of the Flies* for older children.

LEARNING AROUND
A CANAL

Canals and waterways used to be the main communication and transport arteries of a country, taking heavy loads of goods and wares to and from important ports, towns and cities. However, as civilisations developed, the vast majority of man-made canals, towpaths and locks began to serve only to satisfy leisure and tourism-based water dwellers.

Visit an historic waterway and unlock the magic of a bygone era.

BEFORE YOU GO...

Try to gain an understanding of the waterway you will be visiting and to share this information with the family so as to wet (whet) their appetites.

Look online for information to read or print out to take with you on the trip. Get the children looking for images, too. Ask them to find images of the waterway in its heyday. Perhaps print some out and try to spot locations on the day. Find a map of a route for you to follow; enthusiasts often will have created and shared information, photographs and annotated maps of walks, together with fascinating stories and anecdotes from the past. Read as much of this information as you can before you head out and it will provide engaging lines of enquiry.

When you are on the way, get youngsters to think about the journey: how far are you going, how many miles/kilometres are you travelling and how long is it going to take? Relate this to travelling the same distance but at a fraction of the speed – 2 or 3 miles per hour. Work out how long it would take you to get to your destination at 'canal speed'.

ENCOURAGING LINES OF ENQUIRY

- Where did (does) the local waterway go to and from?
- What are the characteristics of a canal?
- How does a lock system work?
- Why did canals fall out of favour and what replaced them?

WHILE YOU ARE THERE...

On arrival at your destination ask the kids to consider how many times they might have asked these questions if they had been travelling at 'canal speed': 'Are we nearly there yet?' or 'Can we stop? I need the toilet.' Encouraging children to empathise with people from the past increases their appreciation of history.

ENCOURAGING DIFFERENT WAYS TO LEARN

Get **TALKING** when you travel through locks. They can be very sociable places, as there is likely to be a lot going on when boats are passing through. Share pleasantries, ask questions and offer help to push or pull the lock gates.

LISTEN out at all times. Some people say we have two ears and one mouth for a reason! Encourage everyone to be aware of the soundscape. It might be motors 'putt-putting', white water rushing into a lock or paddles or oars slapping the surface. Or it might be the natural sounds of the waterway: waterfowl 'chattering' or shouting, fish 'plopping' as they rise and fall, or the gentle rustling of leaves.

HIRE a kayak or take one with you so that the more energetic family members can get out and about at water level. Or do some fishing or cycle the towpath.

SUGGESTIONS
- Carry out **RESEARCH** into locks, viaducts and aqueducts: all are fascinating in their own right.
- **MAKE** a boat of any kind and test how much weight it can carry before it sinks. Try other boat designs too.
- **DRAW** an illustration of a lock, explaining how it works.
- **DESIGN** a leaflet to promote waterways and canals to families.

TIPS
- Get the kids onto the water if you can. Daily boat hire is usually an option.
- Stop and talk to people off and on the water.
- Try to visit a lock or an aqueduct as this will raise the excitement levels of your youngsters.

LEARNING AROUND
A CAVE

Caves are naturally occurring hollow areas under the ground in hillsides or cliffs. The difference between a cave and a hole is that a cave is deep enough to not allow light inside. Caves can vary in size from single chambers to interconnecting passageways and are formed by a range of different geological processes.

BEFORE YOU GO...

There are four main types of cave formation: caves made by rainwater – the acid in the water erodes the rock and eventually forms a hollow; sea caves that are formed by the force of waves crashing into the cliff; lava caves; and glacial caves. When choosing a cave to visit, find out what type of cave it is. Look online at different caves. Some have virtual tours that allow you to explore inside without even going there; this is convenient when they are situated on the other side of the world!

Think about what it will be like inside the cave. Will it be wet or dry? Will it be cold? Talk about how caves were/are used for shelters – what signs might still be there today? If visiting a commercial cave, find out its opening times and when tours might be taking place on the day of your visit.

ENCOURAGING LINES OF ENQUIRY

- How was the cave formed?
- What has the cave been used for?
- Is there evidence of past or present human or animal activity or even plant life in the cave?
- Is the cave interconnected with others and does it lead to other exit points?

WHILE YOU ARE THERE...

Turn your visit to a cave into an adventure. Take on the role of adventurers exploring an unknown world, or speleologists studying new cave formations, or historians hunting out signs of ancient human activity.

ENCOURAGING DIFFERENT WAYS TO LEARN

LOOK around for signs of life. Troglobionts are creatures that live in caves. The word comes from the Greek words *troglo*; meaning 'cave' and *bio* meaning 'life'. See if you can spot any small cave-loving spiders or insects.

LOOK for cave formations such as stalactites and stalagmites – mineral deposits left on the ceiling or floor that form pillars.

LISTEN for the sound of water. Rainwater seeps into the ground and drips into the cave. Some caves contain underground rivers, waterfalls or lakes.

Take a tour and **EXPLORE** the cave, walking and crawling through the subterranean world.

ASK questions and **READ** information about the history of the cave, who has used it and how.

TIPS
- Take torches/head torches so you can see clearly when inside.
- Take spare clothing because the temperature in caves is often noticeably cooler than outdoors.
- Wear sturdy waterproof shoes that provide grip because caves can be damp and slippery.
- Check if you have to book any tours before you get there.
- Stay close to anxious children that might feel claustrophobic or nervous about the dark.

SUGGESTIONS
- **MAKE** your own paint. Grind minerals or crush materials like berries or dirt and mix them with water. Experiment to see what colours you can create.
- **CREATE** your own cave painting. Imagine that you lived in prehistoric times. Scrunch up a piece of brown paper (bag/parcel wrapping). Paint a simple picture using earthy colours, for authenticity.
- **MAKE** your own stalactites and stalagmites. Fill two cups with hot tap water and dissolve as much baking soda (or salt or sugar) into the water as possible. Place a piece of wool between the two cups. Weigh the wool down by attaching a paper clip to each end in the cup. Place a saucer between the cups. Leave and check regularly to see how the stalactites and stalagmites are forming.

LEARNING AROUND
A LIGHTHOUSE

When asked, most people would be able to picture a lighthouse in their mind's eye and it would probably look very similar to everyone else's picture: a red and white-striped tapered tower with a light and lens on the top, yes? But lighthouses are centuries old and have not always looked like this. In fact, they have a rather illuminating past to explore.

BEFORE YOU GO...

It's more exciting for children to visit a lighthouse that is in working order, and even better if it is one that they can enter, rather than visiting an old relic of a bygone age. But a quick glance back into the past will enlighten them about the original purpose and design of the lighthouse. Some principles remain today, even if the structures and lighting technology have changed massively. Spend some time looking up and reading about ancient lighthouses and their role in marking entrances to ports, and how the raising of the fire – the only light source of the time – enhanced the visibility of the light. Ancient lighthouses were not originally intended to warn against dangerous reefs or protruding landmasses, unlike the modern-day equivalents. Modern lighthouses have an additional purpose, which is to enable sailors to locate their position.

Before you visit the lighthouse, get a sense of its location. Why is it there, at that particular spot? Plan to be around when the lighthouse comes to life in the evening, as well as during the day, since there is something magical in seeing the beam of light reaching out to sea.

ENCOURAGING LINES OF ENQUIRY
- What is the history behind the lighthouse? Has the lighthouse always been there?
- Is the lighthouse 'manned'? Why were lighthouses always manned in the past?
- What modern technological advances have taken place over the years, and what has their impact been?
- Does every lighthouse flash in the same way?

WHILE YOU ARE THERE...

A visit to a lighthouse may not be an all-day event, unless it is a special occasion and there are other things going on, but if you can, do try to see the lighthouse in the daytime as well as when it's dark (even if from a distance).

ENCOURAGING DIFFERENT WAYS TO LEARN

LOOK at the lighthouse's flash pattern. This is obviously best done during darkness. Is the pattern regular? What is the pattern? Why do lighthouses have a particular flash pattern?

ASK a member of staff about the role of a lighthouse keeper, today and in the early days. What were the duties and what was life like for keepers, particularly those in remote locations or even out at sea?

SKETCH the outside of the lighthouse, concentrating on its features and structure.

CLIMB to the top of the lighthouse and count the number of stairs. Imagine being a lighthouse keeper before oil or electric lamps were invented.

LOOK around the lighthouse and its museum for a lighthouse poem or sea shanty. Find out what a shanty was and why they were popular with mariners. See if you can learn and sing one or even write your own poem or sea shanty.

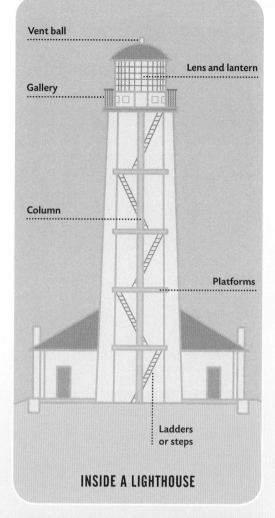

Vent ball

Lens and lantern

Gallery

Column

Platforms

Ladders or steps

INSIDE A LIGHTHOUSE

TIPS
- Check when the lighthouse is open to the public.
- If it's a nice day, take a picnic as lighthouses usually have wonderful vistas.
- When outside and around the clifftops, take care and obey all signage.

SUGGESTIONS
- TRACE the sketch you did at the lighthouse and draw the internals of the lighthouse as you remember it during the tour.
- With a torch and three flat mirrors, EXPERIMENT with the best arrangement for making a fixed light source visible. Try using a flexi mirror or bendable reflective surface.

LEARNING AROUND
A WATERFALL

There are many well-known waterfalls around the world, famous for their record-breaking heights and dramatic scenery. But there are also hidden gems, tucked into hillsides, that are equally as impressive and more accessible. A waterfall will provide a spectacular backdrop for a family day out as well as stimulus for plenty of wonderful, wet work!

BEFORE YOU GO...

Bear in mind recent weather conditions. The volume of water travelling over a waterfall will increase and decrease according to the amount of rainfall that has ocurred. Consider choosing a rainy day, or a day after there has been a lot of rainfall in order to guarantee a more dramatic waterfall.

When choosing where to go, look at online maps to find obscure waterfalls, then make it an adventure to discover them; there might be a short trek to get there, so enjoy the scenery.

ENCOURAGING LINES OF ENQUIRY

- How unspoilt is it? Are there positive or negative signs of human intervention?
- Where has the water coming over the waterfall travelled from?
- What vegetation, if any, is growing around the waterfall?

WHILE YOU ARE THERE...

When you arrive at the waterfall, soak up the atmosphere before getting soaked! Listen to the noise of the falling water; you might even hear it on your approach, as you arrive. Check to see if there is access behind the waterfall so you can slip behind it..

ENCOURAGING DIFFERENT WAYS TO LEARN

WALK up the stream towards the waterfall. Observe the route that the water takes and how the rocks have been shaped and eroded by the flow of the water. Look out for any fish or other signs of life.

STAND/SWIM in the plunge pool. The temperatures might be shocking but will demonstrate how the water that has travelled fresh from the hills, down tributaries to the waterfall and onwards, as running water, therefore is much colder than still water.

LOOK at the stone at the top of the waterfall. Find out what type of rock it is and observe how the power of the water has eroded grooves and channels into it. Pay attention to the rock at the bottom of the waterfall, too. Has it been eroded or shaped by the water over a period of time?

TEST the strength of the falling water by throwing floating objects (e.g. leaves) onto the water and seeing how quickly the ripples carry them away from the falling force.

SUGGESTIONS

- **CREATE** a graph showing the height of the waterfall that you visited. Find out the height of other waterfalls and add them to your graph to make a comparison.
- **MAKE** a papier mâché model of the waterfall. Once dry, add water for the full effect.
- **INVESTIGATE** the strength of falling water. Fill a jug with water and pour it from different heights into the bath. Place a toy boat or similar underneath and see if you can sink it. Treat it as a science experiment (as well as a bit of fun) and be systematic in your methods if you can.

TIPS

- Take waterproofs and expect to get wet. Wear sturdy shoes since the rocks near a waterfall are always slippery.
- Take swimming costumes (and wetsuits, if you're not bold enough to brave the cold water without them).

LEARNING AROUND
A RESERVOIR

Reservoirs are large repositories of water such as lakes that are used to store and supply clean, fresh drinking water to populations of people. Reservoirs can be natural or man-made, such as when a river valley is deliberately dammed and flooded.

Being essentially outdoor environments, reservoirs are perfect for an active day visit and a mix of activity and exertion, as well as purposeful and meaningful learning, often with an environmental, or eco, theme.

BEFORE YOU GO...

Reservoirs serve an important function in the supply and treatment of clean water, so this should form an important element of your visit. Don't worry about having to do much preparation, though, such as learning about the mechanics and technicalities of the infrastructure. Most reservoirs will have some sort of educational provision: a visitor centre and/or information boards. Some may even have a member of staff on hand to answer questions or offer explanations. It might be a good idea to help your children have a grasp of volume, particularly knowing roughly how much water is in a litre or a gallon. Information boards and water gauges may present volumes and levels in either unit of measurement.

Some prior awareness of the global water situation would be useful to develop ahead of a visit. A basic understanding of droughts and floods, unclean water and illness, and how important clean water is to survival will give children an appreciation of water and its value.

Another angle to consider when you are looking to visit a reservoir is whether there is an interesting historical angle to explore. If the reservoir is the result of a flooded river valley, there may be a flooded village at its bottom and there is likely to be information boards or perhaps even a museum to visit linked to this. Similarly, the reservoir may have a connection with a film taken at its location, or even a connection with one of the World Wars – the bouncing bomb was invented by Barnes Wallis and its capacity to bounce was tested on a reservoir in the Peak District. Look for any military connections, as this is likely to capture the interest of children.

ENCOURAGING LINES OF ENQUIRY
- Why and how was the reservoir created?
- How does the level of the reservoir reflect the recent/long-term weather patterns, e.g. a wet winter or a dry summer?
- Beyond water supply and treatment, what other roles does the reservoir have?
- What are the basic principles behind the water supply and treatment systems and processes?

TIPS
- Visit at different times of the year. The reservoir will take on different forms (colour/water level/visitor numbers).
- Check whether dogs and kids can enter the water or get active on it and go prepared.
- Look out for guided ranger walks and local events that may be happening.

WHILE YOU ARE THERE...

There's a lot that can be learned from a distance, so explore the local walks and bike trails that allow you to see the reservoir from different perspectives: low down, high up, and even in and on!

Also, it is surprising but true that reservoirs and their water level marks and lines can help children learn about contour lines that they see on maps.

ENCOURAGING DIFFERENT WAYS TO LEARN

WALK, RUN, CYCLE, PADDLE or **SAIL** the perimeter of the reservoir; this will give you a proper grasp of its scale (as well as give you some outdoor exercise).

LOOK for evidence that you have actually visited a reservoir and not just a lake. A reservoir will have pipes, valves and sluices around and about it. They may be well hidden, so look carefully and spot as many as you can.

TALK to a ranger and learn about water supply and water conservation.

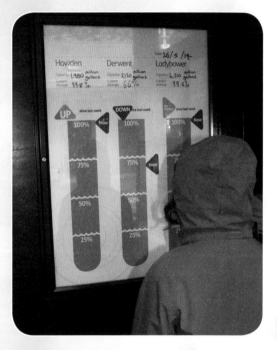

SKIM different shapes and sizes of stones and try different speeds and angles of incidence to see which results in the best skim. Barnes Wallis had to do similar tests when he was developing the bouncing bomb on Derwent reservoir.

TAKE some water and then **MAKE** fake sewerage (as realistic as you can out of all of the things that might get flushed down a toilet or poured down a sink) and then try to filter it to make the water as clean as you can.

FEED the birds with the right food: birdseed or wholegrain bread **NOT** white or brown bread as this can lead to an incurable disease called angel wing.

ODD ONE OUT – FIND THE FAKE FACT!
- ✗ The Aswan Dam in Egypt is situated across the River Aswan.
- The Teton Dam in the USA failed and broke in 1976 when it was being filled for the first time.
- Barnes Wallis' bombs were successfully used to destroy dams in the Ruhr Valley during World War II.
- The Derbyshire village of Derwent was 'drowned' when the Ladybower Reservoir was formed.

BE BOLD
Look out for anyone feeding white or brown bread to ducks, geese or swans and make them aware of angel wing. Let them know that only birdseed or wholegrain bread should be used.

SUGGESTIONS
- CALCULATE the volume of a bath. Fill it manually using litre/pint bottles to see how good your estimate was.
- RECYCLE a plastic bottle and make a rain catcher for your garden. Put a scale on the side and monitor how the water level changes over the year. Consider how the water level of the reservoir you visited might be fluctuating too.
- Put a 'brick' in your toilet flush system to save water. WORK OUT how much it saves per flush, per day, per week and per year. And make sure you get permission first.
- MAKE an Angel Wing Awareness poster, laminate it and then display it by a pond or a lake in the park in your local area.

WHEN YOU GET BACK...

Keep an eye and ear out for announcements that link directly or indirectly to water supply, e.g. hose pipe bans, leakage and burst pipes, etc. Draw attention to these as well as water-related news and issues on a global scale, e.g. drought, flooding or pollution.

COUNTRY LIFE

LEARNING AROUND
A CHILDREN'S FARM

Children usually have a natural attraction to animals and a fascination for small or big, cute or not so cute varieties. In fact, it's not just children that like animals, is it? Adults and even teenagers (although they are not likely to admit it) are likely to enjoy a trip to a children's farm and a chance to learn about the animals that grow and breed there, as well as the ones that possibly even end up on our plates at mealtimes.

BEFORE YOU GO...

Give your children an informal quiz about farm animals and where foods like bacon, sausages, beefburgers, eggs and cheese come from. You might be surprised at how much or how little they know. Young children might not know what an aubergine (eggplant) or a butternut squash is, but children should be able to tell you the basics about common farm animals and their role in the agriculture/food industry.

City farms are extremely important in giving urban children first-hand and hands-on experiences of touching, holding and even milking and feeding farm animals. Without such experiences children are detached from the natural world and the notion of where their food comes from, as well as lacking empathy and care around animals and their welfare.

Children familiar with farms and farm animals can be encouraged to find out about the role the farm plays in the community or about the breeding programme the farm may have, especially if it has any rare breeds.

With quiz complete and lines of enquiry at the ready, head out and have fun, but don't forget your wellies.

ENCOURAGING LINES OF ENQUIRY
- What do the different animals eat?
- Why are the animals in certain fields/pens and not mixed?
- Are free-range eggs in supermarkets really free-range?
- Why are some farms called organic farms?

TIPS

- When the children have had a good old run around after arriving, reign them in a bit and get them to focus on what it is they have come to learn about.
- Take some change for animal food and ensure that the right animals get the right food.
- Take along an antibacterial hand gel for instant cleansing.
- Take some short video clips to use in follow-up tasks.

WHILE YOU ARE THERE...

Initially, let the children be fully free-range and let their sense of excitement and interest lead them (and you). Let them run about in the fresh air and in the big open space that the farm offers – space that your garden is most likely lacking. The children need to be respectful of other people, of course, as well as the animals themselves, but don't be tempted to quash the raw excitement they will experience, especially if it is their first time on a farm.

ENCOURAGING DIFFERENT WAYS TO LEARN

Make sure you take time to **SMELL** the air on a farm – some of it is not so pleasant! But these smells are natural. More natural in fact than most of our day-to-day smells such as air fresheners or fabric conditioner. Find where the smelliest pong is and what is causing it. Think about what we humans smell like to the farm animals.

Get children to **LISTEN** out for the animal sounds that they have been familiar with from a young age, then put their knowledge to the test: takes turns putting a blindfold on and being lead around the farm using the sense of hearing to identify animals.

Encourage children to **QUESTION** the staff on the farm about what goes on there. They will be used to answering questions and are used to dealing with inquisitive children, so allow your children to be bold and ask questions. Get them to feed back their answers to you so that you can genuinely learn something from them; kids like to think they know more than their parents.

Where possible, **TOUCH** or stroke as many animals as you can. Some farms allow you to handfeed baby animals, so check the farm's signage. If your children are apprehensive, encourage them to do what they are comfortable with, but a more physical experience will turn out to be more memorable.

ODD ONE OUT – FIND THE FAKE FACT!
- Cows can see almost 360° around themselves.
- ✗ Goats cannot swim.
- Pigs are omnivores.
- Scientists think that chickens are the closest living relative to the *Tyrannosaurus rex*.

BE BOLD
Challenge the youngsters to choose and learn about an animal. Set the task of sharing their knowledge with 10 other people.

WHEN YOU GET BACK...

Next time you are in the supermarket, look more carefully at the produce on sale and more critically at the labelling. What do you notice about the pricing? Is it morally correct that the meat and eggs from animals that have had an outdoor-reared/organic life are sold at a higher price?

Were there any lines of enquiry that triggered further interest that could be followed up?

SUGGESTIONS
- **PHILOSOPHISE** an unanswerable question, e.g. which came first, the chicken or the egg?
- **CREATE** a map of the farm and colour code the different areas where the animals are. Do your own version with animals that you would have in your farm.
- **MAKE** and edit a 'Talking Heads' video about farm animals with a funny voice-over from the animal's viewpoint.
- **INVENT** a crossbreed based on the food that it would produce, e.g. a Full English.

LEARNING AROUND
A VALLEY

A valley is a general term used to describe the lower, flatter area of land between hills or mountains. Other words include: dale, dell, glen, gorge and ravine. Valleys are usually categorised according to their shape: V-shaped with a river running through and steep sides, or U-shaped with steep sides and a flat floor that has been bulldozed by glaciers. The valley floor may be wooded, have a river run through it or house lakes, reservoirs or even houses.

BEFORE YOU GO...

Spend time locating the valley that you are going to visit on a map. Look at the contour lines on the map. Point out that contour lines show how high the land is, joining together places of the same height. When looking at a map, the contour lines help us to visualise hills and valleys; lines that are close together show land that is steep and contour lines that are further apart show flatter areas of land. Predict what the shape of the valley will look like from the contour lines on the map.

Carry out some research about how valleys are formed. Watch videos that illustrate how the land can be shaped by the sheer force of water or by glacial movement.

ENCOURAGING LINES OF ENQUIRY
- How was the valley formed? Was it eroded by flowing water or carved by glaciers millions of years ago?
- How is the valley used and who by?
- What vegetation is able to grow at different heights and why?

WHILE YOU ARE THERE...

To fully appreciate a valley, get a view from above. Walk up the hills on the side and look down at the valley floor. Look down the length of the valley to see if it makes a V- or U-shape.

ENCOURAGING DIFFERENT WAYS TO LEARN

WALK a cross-section of the valley from one hillside to another. **LOOK** at the different changes in landscape as the land becomes steeper or flatter. What is able to grow or not? Why?

LOOK closely at the map of the valley and identify features within it. Match the map symbols with what is in front of you.

Find the most dramatic view, **PHOTOGRAPH** it and do a sketch of it.

IDENTIFY examples of geotropism (trees growing vertically even though they are on a slope).

LOOK at the houses in the valley (if there are any). Most will be located in the base of the valley where the land is flatter. Building houses on a slope is difficult – can you think why? How would you overcome the issues of the slope when building a house? Look for the highest house in the valley and identify features that have helped to locate it on the slope.

EMPATHISE with what it must be like to live in the valley. What might it be like in winter? How much light does the valley get? Is it accessible?

SUGGESTIONS

- **DRAW** the cross-section that you walked, then label the different features that you identified while you were walking.
- Use your sketch and your photograph to **PAINT** a finished image.
- **MAKE** an adventure flyer of activities that you could do in the valley.

TIP
Wear sturdy walking shoes that support your feet when walking.

LEARNING AROUND
A VINEYARD/ORCHARD/FRUIT FARM

It is easy to buy fruit from a supermarket or grocer without thinking about where it came from. Many children will not associate a packaged product with the process that it has gone through to get to them. A punnet of strawberries or a bag of apples might have a label clearly displaying the farm that it came from, but a visit to an orchard, a vineyard or a fruit farm provides a valuable insight into what goes into growing the fruits that we all love to eat, as well as some tasty treats to take home, too.

BEFORE YOU GO...

There are a range of different fruits that grow in small and large farms at different times of the year. The most fruitful time (no pun intended) will be during the summer and autumn (fall) months – depending on the crop – when the fruits are ready to be picked. A visit at no matter what time of the year will hopefully provide a learning opportunity about the work involved to help the fruits grow successfully.

Have an initial discussion to find out what everyone knows about the fruit and how it grows. You might get some surprising answers that lead to a bank of questions to take with you on your visit. Think about the objective of the visit (not just to buy and eat fruit) and what you want to know by the end. Add to your list of questions if necessary.

There are hundreds and thousands of different species of each fruit, so find out the names of some native species that might be growing at the orchard, vineyard or fruit farm that you are going to visit.

Prior to your visit, take a trip to the local shop and carry out some research. How much does a bag of apples or punnet of strawberries cost? How many do you get for your money? Why do some cost more than others? How are they presented to the customer?

> ### ENCOURAGING LINES OF ENQUIRY
> - How has the farm diversified?
> - What are the main threats to the crops that grow on the farm?
> - What is its carbon footprint? How far does it send the fruit away to sell?
> - Does it use pesticides to aid the growth of its fruits?

TIPS

- Find out if the farm offers tours (more and more do these days) and if you need to book.
- Check to see if you are able to PYO – pick your own.

WHILE YOU ARE THERE...

As well as exploring the grounds of where the fruits grow, use the opportunity to talk to the experts and find out how to be a successful fruit grower.

ENCOURAGING DIFFERENT WAYS TO LEARN

ESTIMATE the weight of any fruit you collect, then **WEIGH** it to see how close you were.

LOOK out for minibeasts and wildlife that are attracted to the vineyard, orchard or fruit farm. How are they helping (or not)?

TASTE test the produce on a farm that grows a range of different fruit (e.g. different types of apples, pears, raspberries or strawberries. Test a blindfolded family member to see if they can identify what they are eating. For added difficulty, try holding your nose and then guessing what the fruit is. This demonstrates how your sense of smell and taste are linked. It is much more difficult to taste anything if you are not using your sense of smell.

TOUCH test a piece of fruit by getting a blindfolded member of the family to see if they can identify a fruit purely by feeling it.

ASK the people that work at the farm about how they look after and grow the crops. Find out where the fruit goes after it leaves the farm.

SEARCH for the biggest fruit. Have a competition to find who can see the biggest strawberry, raspberry, apple or pear etc.

ODD ONE OUT – FIND THE FAKE FACT!

- Cucumbers are fruits.
- Apples, pears, plums and strawberries are members of the rose family.
- ✗ Bananas are also known as 'butter fruit' because of their buttery texture.
- Kiwi fruits contain more vitamin C than oranges.

BE BOLD

- Speak to someone who works at the vineyard, orchard or fruit farm. Take along some prepared questions and interview them about their jobs. Ask for some tips about how to grow fruit successfully.
- Offer to help out picking the fruit.

WHEN YOU GET BACK...

You may return laden down with fruit that you can cook creatively. Go to the kitchen and experiment with recipes but after the eating is done, don't forget to follow up the learning.

SUGGESTIONS

- COOK or BAKE a delicious treat using the fruit that you collected. Have a look at different recipes or make up your own.
- INVENT a *Wallace and Gromit*-style fruit picker that does all the hard work for you.
- PLANT your own fruit tree or bush. Find out the best growing conditions – where and when to plant it – and make sure you continue to take care of it.
- FIND OUT which fruits are grown in other countries. What are the similarities or differences?
- THINK of as many different ways as possible to crush a grape. If you think your ways are weird, some people do it with their feet!

LEARNING AROUND
HILLS AND MOUNTAINS

What's the difference between a hill and a mountain you might ask? It's a simple question, but unfortunately there isn't a simple answer! This is because there is no standardised definition; it is very subjective and often regional. A hill of height X in one area of the country may be deemed a mountain in another region – and vice versa.

It is actually more useful to make your own definition of a mountain by looking for some specific features, like an obvious summit or the steepness of the ground leading up to the summit, and it being noticeably higher than the land around it.

BEFORE YOU GO...

From a young age children will have heard of Mount Everest, the world's highest mountain. It rises 8,848m (29,029ft) above sea level and was unspoilt and unconquered until 1953, when Sir Edmund Hillary and Sherpa Tenzing successfully completed the first ascent. It is now estimated that around 4,000 people have climbed it.

As with Everest, walking or climbing up your chosen hill or mountain will involve you making an ascent that takes you further above sea level. Geographically, heights and elevations are measured above the average height of one or more of the surfaces of the Earth's oceans. In fact, the height above sea level of the summit (the highest point of a hill or mountain) is often used to help define a mountain from a hill. Often, anything over 600m (1,968ft) is considered to be a mountain but as per above, there are no guarantees!

As you make your ascent, you may experience difficult walking conditions or changeable weather. It is therefore very important to make sure you are well prepared and kitted out with the right sort of protective clothing.

If you are not ready to scale a mountain, look instead for a hill fort to visit. The earthworks and fortifications there are interesting and, by the very nature of what they were and why they were built, you are likely to experience an impressive view.

Hill figures are also good to visit and offer another angle – and motivation – to visit and ascend a hill. Predominantly designed to be viewed from an approach, these visual representations are impressive in scale and well worth visiting with children as a stimulus for understanding and revealing ancient folklore and mystery.

ENCOURAGING LINES OF ENQUIRY
- What formed the hill/mountain?
- Are there signs of human interaction (past or present)?

WHILE YOU ARE THERE...

A trip to a hill or a mountain is not complete without a walk or climb to the summit, so factor this into your visit and allow plenty of time to ascend and descend. Take some lunch with you and eat while you have your head in the clouds, literally.

ENCOURAGING DIFFERENT WAYS TO LEARN

IDENTIFY some of the hill/mountain fauna and flora. At different times of the year you'll see different things: in the summer look for butterflies and lizards; look up in the air, too, for birds of prey and the singing summer skylark.

SLEEP on a hill and enjoy a 'billion-star' room, with a view to remember. On a calm and clear summer's evening, drag an adult up to the summit for a stargazing extravaganza. All you need is a head torch, a sleeping bag, a roll mat, a bivvy bag and some snacks and drinks.

LOOK out for interesting geographical features, such as: a ridge (a long narrow top between hills/ mountains); scree (loose pieces of broken rock); a slope (side of the hill); a gorge (steep valley between two mountains); tree line (level at which the trees stop); a cairn (a pile of stones that mark the summit or an important viewing point); and the summit (the top). Make references to these features when you are telling someone about your ascent and they will think you are a gnarly mountaineer!

RESPECT the landscape and the habitat, and lead by example by picking up and 'bagging' any litter you find. You'll then go home happy that you have left the hill/mountain in a better state than you found it.

ODD ONE OUT – FIND THE FAKE FACT!
- Some of the largest mountains are at the bottom of the sea.
- ✗ A chain or group of mountains is known as a string.
- The height of Mount Everest is changing each year.
- Half of the world's fresh water originates from mountains.

BE BOLD
Say 'Hello' to 10 people that pass you when you are out walking or climbing. Even bolder, stop and have a conversation with someone!

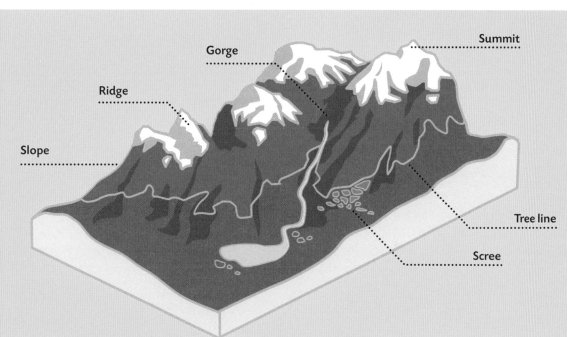

Summit

Gorge

Ridge

Slope

Tree line

Scree

MOUNTAIN TERMINOLOGY

WHEN YOU GET BACK...

When you get back or even on the way back, recognise the effort and 'never-give-up' attitude shown by your young hill walker/mountaineer. It takes determination and strength of character to accomplish a physical feat, even though at the time it might feel like torture! See if you can get them to commit to another hill or mountain challenge in the future.

SUGGESTIONS
- Find a map of your local area and **LOOK** for spot heights and contours to identify different hills and mountains that you could climb.
- **FIND** out more about modern-day Everest 'tourism' and consider the human impact on the environment and the local people.
- **MAKE** an awareness poster of the need to be prepared when out on hills and mountains and include a must-have kit list for people considering climbing a mountain.

LEARNING AROUND
A MINE/QUARRY

Natural materials such as coal, salt, stone and metals are all extracted from the Earth via mines and quarries. This practice has been going on for centuries, ever since prehistoric times. People rely on extracting minerals and materials from the ground even today, but mining is now a less-common profession and many mines worldwide are no longer used due to demand, safety issues or alternative materials.

What is the difference between a mine and a quarry? They both involve extracting materials, but at a quarry the work is done at the surface whereas mining happens underground.

BEFORE YOU GO...

You can't just walk into a working mine or quarry believe it or not, so consider the best place to visit within easy access to you. The obvious choice is to book an educational tour, which many mines and quarries offer. Disused mines and quarries that have been converted into museums also offer guided tours that give an insight into how they were used in the past.

Nowadays, a visit to a mine or quarry is very different to what it would have been over a century ago. In Victorian times, the whole family would have worked in the mines and children would have played an important role. When visiting a mine, spend some time finding out about the jobs that children did. Compare their lifestyle with that of a modern child.

Before going to visit a mine or quarry, find out how much everyone knows. What kind of things are actually mined? Many people know that coal is mined, but there are plenty more materials that we extract from our planet. See if you can draw up a list of as many different materials as possible. Create a family game to see who can guess whether a material is mined or quarried.

Extracting materials from the ground involves a lot of equipment. Try a problem-solving task: discuss how to remove gems from a mine, thinking about which tools would be needed to remove the gems and carry them out. Then find out if you were right. Did you forget anything important? This thinking activity should get the whole family finding out about the process and the difficulties and the dangers that are involved, before actually witnessing and hearing about them on a visit.

ENCOURAGING LINES OF ENQUIRY

- What is the environmental impact of quarrying and mining? Are there alternatives?
- How safe were/are mines and quarries?
- What role did children play in the mine or quarry in the past?
- What are the materials that are/were extracted used for?

TIPS
• A working mine or quarry can have dangers or hazards that everyone in the family should be aware of. Do not wander out of designated areas.
• Tread carefully.

WHILE YOU ARE THERE...

There may be little freedom to explore when visiting a mine or quarry that provides a tour, but don't rely solely upon the information given to you. Encourage the children to ask questions and dig a little deeper (excuse the pun).

ENCOURAGING DIFFERENT WAYS TO LEARN

EMPATHISE with workers in the mines by getting hands-on. Take in the sounds, sights and smells of a mine or quarry and, if available, get your hands dirty touching equipment.

MEASURE the height and width of the mines at different points and compare. Think about how this would have affected people working in it.

GET PHYSICAL by walking, ducking and crawling through the mines.

ASK questions about the dangers of mines in the past and today. Find out how they overcame/overcome them.

LISTEN to the noises of a mine or quarry. If you have an app on a smartphone, try to record how loud the working mine/quarry is.

ODD ONE OUT – FIND THE FAKE FACT!

- The oldest known mine, named 'Lion Cave', is 43,000 years old and is found in Swaziland.
- Gold and copper were the first metals to be found by man in 5000 BC.
- ✗ Africa is the only continent where steel is mined.
- The Ancient Egyptians extracted stone for building massive monuments such as tombs and pyramids.

BE BOLD

Challenge someone at the mine or quarry that you are visiting to play your mine or quarry game. See how many they get right – are you impressed or not?

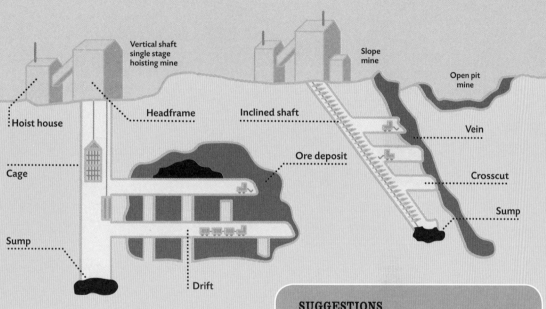

THE WORKINGS OF A MINE

WHEN YOU GET BACK...

After researching the history of mining and quarrying, then experiencing a visit to one or both, follow up any questions that arise. It is surprising what a visit can trigger: further historical research, geological studies or an interest in human and physical geography.

SUGGESTIONS

- MAKE a leaflet explaining the dangers and raising awareness of disused mineshafts.
- FIND OUT about fracking. Is this a good or a bad alternative?
- CREATE your own mine tour in Minecraft. Think about how you can provide your visitors with information about the mines and the materials within it.
- RESEARCH child labour in modern times. Children in the UK worked in mines and factories until the late 19th century, but many children all over the world still have to work rather than benefit from a school education.

LEARNING AROUND
A NATURE RESERVE

Nature reserves are protected areas that are considered important for conservation and research purposes. They are valuable places to take children, abundant as they are with wildlife and people who value wildlife and conservation and who are great role models.

Don't feel that you have to be an expert or have special equipment to visit a nature reserve. If you go as a beginner and are willing to interact and learn from others, you are sure to receive a warm welcome. People at these kinds of places, whether volunteers, members or visitors, are usually happy to help others, particularly if they can tell that you share their passion.

BEFORE YOU GO...

As with any visit, a bit of pre-visit preparation is always worth investing in. Look at the website of the reserve you are to visit, as well as photographs other visitors have taken. Read the key information explaining the conditions you might expect (which will be dependent to some extent on the time of year you visit), and look out for any events they might be running, e.g. a guided walk with a ranger or volunteer.

It's important that you go prepared with the right kit, too. If you are visiting a salt marsh reserve, you'll need some stout footwear and warm layers to protect you from any sea breeze. Whereas, if you are visiting a forest nature reserve, you might want to pack some mosquito spray and wear long trousers to avoid scratched and nettled ankles.

The preparation of the youngsters is as important as the practical preparations. If a child knows where they are going and why, they will engage in and feel more ownership of the visit than if they were just transported somewhere. Without such knowledge, they lack the context needed to take in

and assimilate the environment. Try to get hold of a leaflet ahead of your trip, or simply print one out from the reserve's website, and use this to spark an interest and conversations about the place they are about to experience.

That way, at least they will have a mental picture and some ideas of what to expect. Better still, they will go forewarned and forearmed with some things they want to find out, together with a handful of questions they would like answering.

ENCOURAGING LINES OF ENQUIRY
- What are the characteristics of this particular nature reserve?
- Why is this particular area protected?
- What are the main threats (human and natural) to this reserve?
- How does the reserve encourage people to value conservation?

TIPS
- Arrive as early as you can so that you can maximise the time you'll have at the reserve.
- Borrow some binoculars or a scope from someone before you go.
- If you have binoculars of your own, remember to take them with you (why not put them in the car right now?).

WHILE YOU ARE THERE...

Try and explore as much of the reserve as you can, but take your time and immerse yourselves as fully as time allows. Stop regularly to observe, discuss and share. And remember, the quieter you can be, the more you are likely to see.

ENCOURAGING DIFFERENT WAYS TO LEARN

LISTEN regularly. This actually means stopping and listening, completely blocking out any external or internal distractions. Focus only on listening for a few minutes or so, then relax and share what you heard. You'll be amazed at the sounds you can hear when you actively listen.

LOOKING is obviously a very important way to learn while at a nature reserve. Encourage children to look at different levels (distances), e.g. a distance view of the landscape, taking in the big picture, contrasted with a macro view of the smallest level of detail possible, such as an insect going about its daily chores.

ASK questions, lots of them, especially when you have access to an 'expert'. An expert may come in the form of a volunteer or a reserve ranger. Encourage your kids to ask other people – unless you view yourself as an expert, that is.

GET ACTIVE Young children will be fascinated with the sounds and movements of the animals they spot and they won't be embarrassed to pretend to be them. So make the most of this to consolidate the learning by getting them to 'be' a chosen animal. View them through the binoculars and say, 'I think I've spotted a ...' to see if you have correctly identified them.

Older kids may just need to let off steam and race around the open spaces there might be. Be respectful of other people and of course the local animal inhabitants, though!

ODD ONE OUT – FIND THE FAKE FACT!

- The world's first modern nature reserve was created in West Yorkshire, England.
- The North East Greenland National Park is the largest protected area in the world.
- The Great Barrier Reef Marine Park contains the largest cluster of corals in the world.
- ✗ The Galapagos Marine Reserve is the largest marine reserve in the world.

BE BOLD

Ask a fellow visitor who looks knowledgeable whether they have spotted anything of particular interest, and if so, could they please point it out to you.

WHEN YOU GET BACK...

Upon returning with pink cheeks after a full day out looking at wildlife, your minds might be buzzing with the information that you have learnt. Can you really remember the names of all the different types of birds, trees, plants and minibeasts you've seen? Don't let the day fizzle away into memories – try to keep it alive with some follow-up activities.

SUGGESTIONS

- **DRAW** the animal or bird that represents the nature reserve. Alternatively, create your own symbol for the reserve.
- **RAISE** money for the nature reserve – have a toy sale or go busking.
- **BECOME AN EXPERT.** If the visit triggered an interest or new-found passion, then go with it. Do further research or join a club that will expand the interest further.
- **CREATE** a test for others in the family to answer. See how much you, and the others, can remember by creating a series of questions about the nature reserve, its location, its habitats and inhabitants.

LEARNING AROUND
A SAFARI PARK/GAME RESERVE

The word 'safari' originates from the Swahili language and means to travel or to journey. The classic safari destination is the continent of Africa where tourists voyage to get sightings of large sub-Saharan animals in their natural settings.

Unfortunately, many animals are endangered due to human activity, so the opportunity to see animals in the wild is rare and often dangerous. Game reserves have been set up to protect the animals and tourists can drive through on safari to get a closer look at them.

BEFORE YOU GO...

Not everyone can afford to travel to Africa for a real safari experience. Luckily, from the 1960s onwards, safari parks began to appear all over the world. They offered people the opportunity to drive their own vehicles through open, natural spaces and enclosures to observe animals as they roamed around freely. Most children love animals and are fascinated by the exotic creatures that originate in faraway countries, so being able to see them from the safety of their own cars is a thrilling experience.

There is a lot to take in on a visit to the safari park, so enjoy seeing as much as possible. Try to focus the children's interest on one particular animal before your visit. Let them choose an animal that particularly appeals. Ask them to become the animal expert (or egghead) and find out specific information about the animal through research, e.g. what is the animal's natural habitat?, how does the animal hunt?, what is the average lifespan in the wild, in comparison to captivity?, is the animal endangered? Get them to prepare notes that they can refer to during the safari drive.

ENCOURAGING LINES OF ENQUIRY

* What does the safari park do to support conservation and raise awareness?
* How natural are the enclosures that the animals are kept in?

WHILE YOU ARE THERE...

Going to a safari park is like going on holiday for the day. Excitement levels will be high so make sure that the day is full and that you don't miss out on any opportunities.

ENCOURAGING DIFFERENT WAYS TO LEARN

Take turns to give an audio tour about your chosen animal using prepared notes as a prompt. **RECORD** the audio tour for later. Photograph and video the animals as you drive around to make a video documentary.

LOOK out for the basic needs of each animal, e.g. shelter, food and water. Where are they?

TALK to keepers about dangers facing animals in the wild, e.g. poaching.

COUNT how many animals there are in the enclosures. Find out if this is a natural number.

LOOK carefully at the security of the enclosures. What materials are used for the fences and why do they vary for different animals?

COMPARE the life expectancy of animals in captivity to those in the wild. Discuss the pros and cons of safari parks versus freedom.

OBSERVE animal's behaviour. Think about the food chain: animals high up the food chain tend to sleep a lot; grazing animals are always eating; small animals are fast etc.

SUGGESTIONS

- **MAKE** a documentary about your chosen animal, combining photos and video footage taken on your visit with the audio tour.
- **CREATE** your own awards ceremony. Award animals according to your own list of criteria by deciding who is the fastest, strongest, ugliest etc.
- **DESIGN** the best safari vehicle. How would you kit out your car if you were going on a real safari? Would you change the sunroof, have bigger windows, have a viewing cage on the roof or an electric motor so you can travel quieter?

TIPS

- Check out times and events for other attractions that are offered at the park.
- Be aware of the safety rules and abide by them when driving through the safari park.
- If you have time, drive around a second time before you have to leave.

LEARNING AROUND
A FOREST/WOODS

'Trees are planet Earth's lungs' according to the saying. Our ancient woodlands and historical relics from days of old are also a kind of living long-term memory bank. They have witnessed hundreds of years of history and the unwritten stories stored within the pulp of trees may be untappable, but the opportunities for youngsters to explore, discover and interpret this history are as vast as some of the grand, ancient trees themselves.

BEFORE YOU GO...

You may know of a local forest or wood that is near to where you live or of one that you have heard about but never visited. Take the opportunity to visit somewhere new if you are on holiday or visiting somewhere for the first time. A woodland is deemed ancient if it has been around since at least medieval times (the 15th century) and will contain a great variety of wildlife and fauna.

Before you head out to your wood of choice, get your heads together and make a list of what you might expect to find there: wildlife, native tree types, season-specific berries or fungi. Record these in a notebook, and take the notebook with you so that you can make a point of trying to find them.

Your chosen woodland is likely to have been around for hundreds of years, and will feature on old maps of the area. Look online for historical maps that feature the woodland; you'll be surprised how interesting this task can be – honest!

Once you know the location of the wood and its age, refresh your history (no, not your browser's history) and consider which historical eras your woodland has witnessed: Roman, Viking, Anglo-Saxon or the Middle Ages. Thinking about the present and the future will lead to considerations about the current pressures on woodland through modern living, climate change or local policy.

Developing some lines of enquiry to explore while you are there will ensure your visit is as rich as the diversity of the forest itself.

ENCOURAGING LINES OF ENQUIRY
- How old is the woodland?
- What animals live there?
- Is the woodland well looked after or protected?
- Are there any historical remains from a past era?
- Is the forest well used by others?
- What is the wood's relationship with any local populations?

WHILE YOU ARE THERE...

Take a notebook and pencil with you into the woodland, as well as your smartphone, to enable you to capture different types of 'evidence' about its traits and features.

ENCOURAGING DIFFERENT WAYS TO LEARN

Regardless of the season, there will be plenty to see. Encourage children to **LOOK** high into the canopy as well as low into the understorey. There will be plenty to see, but the harder you look the more will be revealed. Record what you discover in your notebook or in your smartphone's camera roll.

Be **MINDFUL.** Find an insect or a leaf and watch it for a minute or so – really watch it. Block out all thoughts and imaginative wanderings and concentrate solely on your chosen subject.

LOOK carefully for unusual mounds or troughs. They may be the remains of a burial ground, or defences.

EXPLORE the smells. Outdoor places are often smelly places, in the nicest sense of the word, so go on an olfactory hunt by literally following your nose! Try and close off all of your other senses and tune into the smells of the woodland. You could even blindfold one of the family and have them lead the rest of you around. On reaching a smelly destination, remove the blindfold and have a chat about the smell. What it's like? What's making it? Why does it smell?

Do some **READING.** Protected woodlands, or those with some historical or cultural significance, will have information boards and notices that you can glean information from. Take photographs, as these may be a good resource to use when following up the visit.

GET PHYSICAL. People who once lived in forests would make shelters from the natural materials, exploiting their waterproof properties and their strength. There is no better way to help children learn about this than having them make their own simple shelter from materials they find around them. Insist that they only use things they find on the forest floor and do not allow them to cut or break anything living.

ODD ONE OUT – FIND THE FAKE FACT!

- Trees are actually just tall plants.
- The oldest tree ever recorded was 5200 years old.
- ✗ Some trees can grow to a massive 1000m (3280ft) in height.
- Growth rings can be used to determine the age of a tree.

BE BOLD

Make a phone call to a forest or woodland charity and ask them how you can help protect a local woodland.

WHEN YOU GET BACK...

When you get home make sure you maintain the momentum of the visit. Print out the best photos of the day and use them, together with any field notes and sketches, to help with some of the suggestions listed.

Plan a return visit at a different time of the year to see how the wood has changed.

SUGGESTIONS

- **CREATE** a collage of the visit using the photographs you took and the notes you made. Stick some leaves around the edge to make a natural border.
- **RESEARCH** shelter constructions and design a shelter to build next time you are in a forest.
- **DRAW** a detailed illustration of an insect or forest animal.
- **MAKE** a bird feeder for wild forest birds.

LEARNING AROUND
A FIELD

So you may be thinking, 'A trip to a field, are you serious?!' But before you dismiss this idea, think: a field is just an open expanse of land, so it could mean you visit a playing field, a meadow, an agricultural field, even an airfield. Interested now? Then read on.

BEFORE YOU GO...

Give your visit some forethought to ensure you get the most out of it. For example, a farmer's field that has just been ploughed over may not have as much potential as a field of stubble and hay bales.

Also, if you just head out without thinking, you might leave without some necessary equipment such as a pooter or magnifying glass (if your focus is to look for minibeasts as part of a habitat study).

The time of the year will also dictate the experience you have and the kinds of things you might expect to see. But don't let the weather put you off visiting a field; just make sure you have the right gear on (boots and waterproofs in wet weather).

If you plan to visit an airfield, look out in the local press for news of events being held. Sometimes airfields are used to host stages of car rallies or car boot sales.

ENCOURAGING LINES OF ENQUIRY

Discuss with your youngster what questions they might have about the field you are going to visit:

- What do they expect will be growing there?
- Do they expect to see any animal activity? If so, what and why?
- Will there be any human activity on display? If yes, what kind?

WHILE YOU ARE THERE...

Make sure your trip is enjoyable and entertaining. Punctuate the learning with fun by allowing the kids to run around and let off steam in the open space, if appropriate. Of course, the learning needs to be fun and informal, too –nothing too heavy or serious!

ENCOURAGING DIFFERENT WAYS TO LEARN

Let the children get their hands muddy and **TOUCH** things. The 'feel' of soil will give you a good clue as to how it is composed. If it feels gritty it probably has a lot of sand in it, whereas clay soil will feel very smooth because the particles are packed together tightly. Something that feels softer than sand but different to clay is a silt-based soil.

LOOK carefully at the wildlife. Get down on your hands and knees, ideally with a magnifying glass, to see what is living close to the ground in the field habitat. Even better, if you have a pooter, then you can collect some minibeasts for closer inspection. See if you can see the individual body segments and legs for: Insects (3 and 6) and Arachnids (2 and 8).

Make a quadrant frame (1m/yd x 1m/yd) out of some thin wood and use this to sample $1m^2/yd^2$ of the field. **COUNT** everything, as much as you can, including different types of grasses, weeds and flowers. Then **MEASURE** the dimensions of the field and scale-up the quadrant findings. This will be a good indication of how diverse the habitat is.

SUGGESTIONS

- **MAKE** a food chain, or food web, for the field habitat you visited.
- **INVENT** a clever way to keep crows, gulls and pigeons off farmers' fields.
- **DECLUTTER** your bedroom and find some toys that are no longer played with, then take them along to a local car boot sale.
- **BUILD** a hibernation hotel for minibeasts out of old wood or sections of bamboo, then leave it in a local hedgerow during the autumn (fall).

TIPS

- Make sure you stick to footpaths and use stiles to get into and out of agricultural fields.
- Discourage children from picking wild flowers (even if they look like weeds), as they may be protected.
- Respect the fact that the field, whatever its kind, is a habitat for a wealth of living things.

LEARNING AROUND
A NATIONAL PARK

National parks are areas of protected countryside where landowners and organisations aim to conserve the landscape, wildlife and cultural heritage of an area of natural beauty. These parks welcome visitors so they, too, can appreciate, learn about and enjoy all that there is on offer. Each national park differs, but, whether it is located on the coast, in woodland or within a mountain region, there is always plenty to do.

BEFORE YOU GO...

National parks want to promote a love of nature and the outdoors so they often offer events, walks or talks throughout the year. Rangers, knowledgeable in their fields, will provide a depth of information that will benefit the whole family. Find out which parks may be appropriate for members of your family and their particular interests. You will probably need to book in advance to guarantee a place and avoid disappointment. There might also be a charge to pay, although some events are free and some encourage you to volunteer some of your time to help support conservation.

Your plans for the day will vary according to the location that you choose. Plan suitable activities for your family and take any necessary equipment, e.g. binoculars, a telescope, a camera, a smartphone etc. It might be a good idea to check the weather conditions if you are considering long walks or stargazing.

ENCOURAGING LINES OF ENQUIRY
- What are the issues and challenges facing the national park?
- How does the national park differ from others in the country or around the world?
- Who lives in the national park and what do they do?
- How do/can the public help or support the conservation of the park?

WHILE YOU ARE THERE...

A day at a national park will be a day in the outdoors. Enjoy the open space and freedom: run, cycle, climb, jump, skip, roll and breathe in the fresh air! Make the most of the walking and cycling trails that a national park has to offer.

ENCOURAGING DIFFERENT WAYS TO LEARN

LOOK at the stars. National parks are renowned for having very little light pollution. Their dark skies provide the perfect location for a spot of stargazing. Stay the night or go after the sun has set and use a telescope or binoculars to try and spot some constellations or look closely at the surface of the Moon.

LISTEN to a talk. Rangers provide informative talks about the landscape and wildlife associated with the park. Tap into their knowledge and **ASK** questions about anything you don't know. Some national parks also offer an audio tour with downloadable podcasts.

EXPLORE the geography of the area through an orienteering challenge. Some national parks have maps and orienteering posts that you need to locate as you wander around the woodland or hillside. This is sometimes referred to as letterboxing. A more high-tech alternative might be geocaching.

LISTEN to and **OBSERVE** closely what there is in the natural environment – go on a nature hunt. Try to spot wildlife or plants associated with the area and look out for native butterflies in hedgerows, reptiles lounging on rocks on hillsides or waterfowl wading on the coastline. Take along a book, fact sheet or app that will help you identify them.

SUGGESTIONS

- **CREATE** your own orienteering challenge in your neighbourhood. Stick up numbers at various locations and mark these on a map. Challenge a family member to find them all. For tech-savvy kids, add **QR** codes at each point, together with questions to answer.
- **RESEARCH** star constellations. Find your birth sign. Budding astronomers could produce a guide of the most common constellations and how to spot them.
- **MAKE** up a mountain bike skills course in your area, which practises fundamental skills such as balance and slow speed control manoeuvrability. These are all useful when out on the national park trails.

TIPS

- National parks often offer appealing extras for visitors such as boat trips and train journeys. Check the costs and running times of these before your planned trip.
- Have some change ready for the car park.
- Be prepared for changes in weather by taking layers and waterproofs with you.
- Try to get there early to appreciate the environment before the crowds descend.

CULTURE
AND ENTERTAINMENT

LEARNING AROUND
A SCULPTURE

Sculptures, or three-dimensional models, are not confined to art galleries and can be found all over, even in the most unusual places. They differ in size, shape and style. They may please you, shock or scare you or simply make you smile.

Sculptures can be temporary or permanent stand-alone pieces of art or one of many displayed on a trail. They aren't always found in rural woodlands and increasingly cities are displaying sculptures to capture the interest of visitors and residents. In London, a selection of brightly coloured elephants or bears have been dotted around in recent years.

BEFORE YOU GO...

Art is very subjective; everyone has personal tastes and what will appeal to one person won't necessarily appeal to another. It will be the same in families. Spend some time looking at images of different sculptures and discuss likes and dislikes. Get the children to express their opinions and attempt to explain why. There are no right or wrong answers, so encourage an open discussion.

When examining images of sculptures look at the materials that have been used to create them. Which materials will be easy to work with and why? Which materials will stand the test of time? Think about which tools a sculptor might have used to carve, mould or construct the finished product. Find pieces of wood and metal and demonstrate how difficult they are to bend or shape.

Choose a sculpture or trail that will appeal to the family and carry out some research beforehand. Find out the name of the sculptor or artists that designed and made the artwork that you will be going to see. Have they done any other pieces of artwork? If visiting a sculpture trail, find out

whether there is a theme and why it was commissioned. Allocate questions to different family members and ask them to find the answers. After a set amount of time, regroup to share your findings.

Prior to visiting your chosen sculpture(s), have a clear sense of what you want to achieve as well as allowing time to appreciate what you are going to see. If you want to create your own artwork or your own guide about the sculpture(s), go with a shared aim of asking questions, finding out information and collecting images.

ENCOURAGING LINES OF ENQUIRY

- Why has the sculpture been made and placed in its current location? Is it celebrating or commemorating an event?
- Does the sculpture or sculpture trail attract many visitors? Why?
- How could the visitor experience be improved?

TIPS

• Find out if there is a map, a tour or information about the sculpture(s) on arrival. If not, have some information up your sleeve (or downloaded) in preparation.

• If visiting a trail, consider the length of the trail and the number of pieces to look at. If you think your children will tire easily or become disinterested before the end, focus on only a few key pieces.

WHILE YOU ARE THERE...

Before embarking on your art appreciation, get a sense of the location. Children might be keen to rush off to the sculpture(s) as quickly as possible, but encourage a slower pace so they can appreciate the artwork from afar as well as up close.

ENCOURAGING DIFFERENT WAYS TO LEARN

LOOK at the sculpture from different angles. You might see details from one angle that you can't from another. Play an I-spy game, challenging other family members to spot interesting things about the sculpture.

READ any information that is provided about the sculpture. Try to sum it up in just a sentence or two.

TALK about your opinion on the sculpture.

LISTEN to others to see if you agree or disagree.

PHOTOGRAPH the sculpture(s) with the aim of displaying them in your own guidebook. If using an app, apply filters and techniques that will enhance the appearance of the image.

EXPLORE the shadow of the sculpture. Discuss how it might look at different times of the day and why. Experiment by changing the shape of the shadow, by standing near or by adding objects close to the sculpture.

ODD ONE OUT – FIND THE FAKE FACT!

- The *Angel of the North* is Britain's largest sculpture.
- ✗ Easter Island is famous for having over **800** stone egg sculptures, carved from solidified volcanic rock.
- The Terracotta Army consists of over **8,000** life-size statues of soldiers.
- The **WEEE** man sculpture, at the Eden Project in Cornwall, represents the amount of electrical waste and electronic equipment that the average British household throws away in a lifetime.

BE BOLD

Be an art critic for the day. Give your opinion on an artwork. Write a brief description of your thoughts and reaction to the sculpture(s) and leave it for others to read.

WHEN YOU GET BACK...

Unleash the budding artist in you. After being inspired by seeing the work of others, have a go at creating your own artwork. Celebrate everyone's individuality and creativity by showcasing your work for others to see.

SUGGESTIONS

- **MAKE** a sculpture guidebook. Using the photographs that you took of the sculpture(s), create a guidebook for other families to read before going on a visit.
- **DESIGN** your own sculpture in keeping with the theme. Get everyone in the family to design their own as well.
- **MAKE** a jigsaw. Print out a photograph of a sculpture and cut it into pieces. Look at other jigsaws and think about how to make yours easier or harder.
- **LEARN** different art techniques. **EXPERIMENT** with different art mediums that you might not have used before. Think about creating sculptures out of papier mâché, ice, sand, paper, wood or even recyclable rubbish that you have collected.
- **MAKE** a sculpture trail from the sculptures that you create. Mark the sculptures on a map for others to follow. Provide information about the sculptures for your audience.

LEARNING AROUND
A STATUE

A statue is a three-dimensional piece of artwork. It differs from a sculpture in that it is always a realistic representation of a person, animal or mythical being. Statues are sculpted, modelled, carved or cast out of hard materials such as stone, wood, clay or metal. Many famous historic figures have had statues made of them.

BEFORE YOU GO...

If you are going to visit the statue of a famous person, it is important to invest some time in finding out about the life of that person. What were they famous for? You may visit statues from a period of history, e.g. Ancient Greeks or Romans. Find out what similarities these statues had.

Statues are usually located outdoors, so therefore the materials that they are made from have to be weather resistant. Have a discussion about all the different materials that statues could be made from and what their properties are. Don't just stick to the obvious ones, but have fun talking about why a statue isn't made from paper or marshmallow, for instance!

ENCOURAGING LINES OF ENQUIRY
- Why was a statue made of the person?
- Why was the statue placed in its current position?
- What effect has the weather or time had on the statue and the material that it is made from?

WHILE YOU ARE THERE...

A visit to a statue may be part of a larger visit to a location, therefore consider how it will fit in. Unless immediately visible upon arrival, treat the trip to the statue as a treasure hunt.

ENCOURAGING DIFFERENT WAYS TO LEARN

TALK to or for the statue. Take on the role of the statue, hiding behind the statue if you can and ask a family member to pose some questions.

LISTEN to some talking statues. In London, 35 statues have become 'talking statues'. Using a smartphone, swipe a plaque and hear famous voices take on the role of the statue.

How realistic is the statue to an actual body? **TEST** out some simple body ratios: an adult femur (thigh bone) is a quarter of a person's height; most people have a 1:3 head to height ratio. Measure the statue and see if it matches these ratios.

LOOK at the material that the statue is made of. How has it stood the test of time? Try to spot signs of erosion from the weather or from hands touching it.

PRETEND to be a statue. How long can you stay still for? What difficult positions can you hold without moving? There are street artists that make a living from dressing up and 'being' statues for the day in public spaces.

MAKE a sundial using the statue. Take some chalk and draw around a distinctive shadow shape on the hour, marking the time. Do this for as many hours as you are there for. Other visitors will then be able to use your sundial to tell the time.

SUGGESTIONS

- **MAKE** your own statue. Using modelling clay, try to make a small statue of yourself or a person of your choice.
- **CREATE** a podcast for a statue. Imagine what the statue would say when you stopped to look at it. Take on the role of the person and record your own voice. Make a QR code for your recording and if you return to the statue, leave it for other people to listen to.
- **MAKE** your sundial in the garden using a stick (instead of the statue) and stones.

TIP
Consider the location of the statue and how to get to it, how far to walk, where to park etc.

LEARNING AROUND
A FESTIVAL/SHOW

There are a range of festivals and shows throughout the year to suit all tastes. The summer months tend to offer the most options understandably, because they predominantly take place in the outdoors. The image of a festival-goer is often a drunken young person, wearing wellies and caked in mud, but this is a false stereotype since families are often welcome at festivals and shows.

Festivals/shows can vary in length; some last a couple of days or an extended weekend whereas some, like the Edinburgh Fringe Festival each August, last for up to three weeks. Common things you could expect to find at festivals and shows you might attend include amazing music, a great selection of food and craft stalls, stages and portaloos.

BEFORE YOU GO...

Choose which festival will appeal to your family. Whether it is a large well-known music, literature or performing arts festival or a select food, adventure, bushcraft or film festival, have a clear idea of what is on offer before you get there. Spend time looking at the festival website if there is one, and any advertising associated with the festival/show. Discuss what everyone in the family wants to see and do.

Some festivals offer hands-on courses. There may be a charge for these and you will more than likely need to book up the course before arriving. Check if you need to take any equipment with you and consider this when you are doing your packing.

If you are staying for more than one day then camping is often an option, but this needs to booked well in advance too. Consider carefully where you will want to pitch your tent. This will ideally be in a family area if there is one, since loud music booming through the canvas late at night might not be so appealing to the smaller members of the family.

Festivals are largely held in the summer; however, a quick check of the weather forecast is always advisable because you never know! A muddy field can be a lot of fun, but you should be prepared for it.

ENCOURAGING LINES OF ENQUIRY
- How green/environmental is the festival or show? What opportunities are there to recycle etc.?
- How does the festival accommodate the large number of visitors?
- Is the festival good value for money?

TIPS
- When planning to go to a festival book well in advance and try to get any available deals to reduce the cost of tickets.
- Stick together and make sure everyone is aware of what to do if anyone gets lost.
- Travel light.

WHILE YOU ARE THERE...

A festival or show can be intimidating when you first arrive, so take in the whole experience before plunging into activities. Wander around and soak up the buoyant atmosphere.

ENCOURAGING DIFFERENT WAYS TO LEARN

LEARN something new. Watch and talk to others to find out how to do a new skill or learn a new piece of information. Make something that can be given as a present to someone when you return.

LOOK at the posters and programmes. How are the performers and events ranked? Do the bigger stars appear in a larger font? Do you agree with the ranking they've been given?

LISTEN to a performance (band, poem, talk etc.) by someone you have never heard of before.

THINK about the costs involved in running a festival. How are the organisers making money and what things will they have to spend money on in order to run the festival/show?

ODD ONE OUT – FIND THE FAKE FACT!

- ✗ Free beer was given out at the first Glastonbury Festival.
- The Edinburgh Fringe Festival is the largest arts festival in the world, lasting three weeks every August.
- The children's version of the Hay Festival is called Hay Fever.
- The original ticket price for the Isle of Wight Festival was £1.25.

BE BOLD

There is always a vast selection of food stalls at festivals and shows offering unusual meat burgers or dishes from other countries. Try to be daring and try some foods that you have never eaten before.

WHEN YOU GET BACK...

When you return from a festival or show reflect on what was good and not so good and if you would want to go again or not. Discuss as a family what everyone enjoyed and how the experience could have been better.

SUGGESTIONS

- DESIGN a logo for the festival/show for next year that represents what it has to offer.
- IMAGINE there was a new family festival. Create an events programme poster showing/explaining what would be there.
- Become an entrepreneur. If you had a stall at the festival /show, what would you sell? MAKE some of your products and test them out on family and friends, e.g. a new brand of sweets, smoothies, jewellery etc.

LEARNING AROUND
A THEATRE/AMPHITHEATRE

An amphitheatre, often associated with Ancient Greek and Roman times, is a circular, open-air performance space with a central area surrounded by tiered seats. The word derives from the Ancient Greek word *amphitheatron* – *amphi* meaning 'on both sides' or 'around' and *theatron* meaning a 'place for viewing'. Although most amphitheatres were man-made structures admired for their architecture, there are also naturally ocurring amphitheatres – performance spaces where natural geology amplifies the sound. Modern open-air theatres are similar to those of Ancient Greek times with the audience sat in an arc around the stage.

BEFORE YOU GO...

So what's the difference between Greek and Roman amphitheatres? Greek amphitheatres had tiered seats in a semicircular formation around the stage, whereas Roman amphitheatres had raked seating that surrounded the performance area, more like a modern-day stadium. Visiting either of these would provide a fascinating family outing.

Before you go to your chosen amphitheatre, find out when it dates from and what it was used for. Carry out some research about the differences and similarities between different amphitheatres; view the amphitheatre on Google Maps; take a virtual tour of the Roman colosseum or an Ancient Greek theatre to gain an insight into what a complete amphitheatre would have looked like; find out what kind of performances would have taken place. They are worth investigating.

For your thespian offspring, ask them to prepare a short performance to be performed at the amphitheatre. Remember to get them to practise before they go.

ENCOURAGING LINES OF ENQUIRY
- What importance does the location of the amphitheatre play?
- How does the seating arrangement help the audience to appreciate a performance?
- What materials were used in the making of the open-air theatre and why?

WHILE YOU ARE THERE...

The magic of theatre that is steeped in history will provide stimulus for a range of learning. As well as getting onto the stage for a spot of performing, there is a lot of scientific and mathematical work that can be done.

....

ENCOURAGING DIFFERENT WAYS TO LEARN

EXPERIMENT with how far sounds can travel in the amphitheatre. Stand in the central performance area and speak at different volumes. See if your audience of family members can hear you from different seats in the auditorium.

INVESTIGATE how voices need to be projected on the stage. Have someone stand on the stage with a tennis ball. Get them to throw the tennis ball to different family members in the audience. More effort will be needed to throw the ball to members that are further away. In the same way the voice needs to be projected further to be heard by those in the back seats.

MEASURE distances of different audience seats from the stage. What is the furthest seat from the stage?

INVESTIGATE ticket prices. If you were selling seats for a performance, how would you price them? Which seats would be the most expensive and why?

BE THEATRICAL! Get onto the stage and perform a song, a dance or a poem. Make sure that it is a polished performance.

WATCH a performance that is taking place at the amphitheatre.

SUGGESTIONS

- How fast does sound travel? Well, we know it travels at the speed of sound, but what is that speed? Try to **WORK IT OUT** for yourself. Have two people stand 500m (1640ft) apart, one with a stopwatch. One person claps their hands and the person with the stopwatch times (to the nearest tenth of a second) how long it takes to hear the sound. Then carry out a simple calculation:

$$\text{Speed of sound} = \frac{\text{distance}}{\text{time}}$$

- **CREATE** a gladiatorial fight sequence to perform to an audience. Stage fighting is practised so that none of the actors are hurt, but should be convincing enough for the audience to believe in it. Consider returning to the amphitheatre to carry out your performance.
- **MAKE**/decorate a mask that could be used in an Ancient Greek theatrical performance. Masks were worn by actors and depicted their characters and emotions, therefore often had exaggerated features.
- **BUILD** a model of an amphitheatre in Minecraft.

TIPS

- Take a camera with you in order to record any performances.
- Find out if there any suitable performances planned at the amphitheatre that you are visiting.

LEARNING AROUND
A FAMOUS LANDMARK

Landmarks were once important as navigational aids and so tended to be large in scale. Nowadays, though, the term can refer to a structure that has become symbolic to a region or place, including buildings and parks.

They can be found in busy built-up places like capital cities or rural and remote areas. Landmarks usually have a local story behind them and finding out the story is part of what makes visiting a landmark so interesting.

BEFORE YOU GO...

If you want a visit to a landmark to be surprising and mysterious, then do little in the way of preparing your child for the visit. If you want the mystery to stimulate some anticipation and excitement, do some prep! Start by establishing the location of the place. Often the landmark's story is related to its location; it could be where a significant event happened or the site of a pilgrimage or festival.

Once you have revealed the story, explore its origins further. It may be that the story takes you back into a community's past or a family history. Or maybe even into the world of legends and mythology. Where it takes you will depend on the landmark you visit.

Obviously the more you know about where you are going, the more you can make it an informative and enjoyable experience for your little ones. If it's a sunny day, make the most of it by taking a picnic or some games to play.

ENCOURAGING LINES OF ENQUIRY
- Who made the landmark? When? Why?
- Where are the materials that it was made out of? Is the construction and the origin of the materials part of its story?
- Is the landmark a commemorative piece? What is it commemorating?

WHILE YOU ARE THERE...

Landmarks are by their very nature impressive places, so take your time to take in as much of the sites, history and atmosphere as possible. Walk around and look for different viewpoints and give the landmark the respect it deserves.

ENCOURAGING DIFFERENT WAYS TO LEARN

MAKE a view dial (like a sundial but it shows the direction and names of things that are visible). With a map and compass,or just a rough idea of the main compass points, and binoculars, record places and features that are in view, and note their distances.

EXPLORE the landmark through a camera lens. Look for interesting views and perspectives that capture the atmosphere and scale of the landmark through a portfolio of different photographs.

BUY a present from the gift shop without spending your own money! Do this by using your powers of persuasion to get your parents to buy it. But here's the catch: you have to persuade them based on how well the gift will remind you of something, or teach you something about the landmark. In other words, the gift must have learning potential!

LISTEN very carefully to the other visitors' conversations as they take place around the landmark. Compile a list of 10 adjectives (describing words such as huge, bright green or eerie) to best describe the landmark.

SUGGESTIONS

- Be a designer. DRAW and describe a new item for the gift shop. Your gift must be original, feasible and commemorate the landmark.
- WRITE a mythical story/tale associated with the landmark. Make it as exciting as possible, and try to base it on some truth.
- Use one of your creative photographs to MAKE a tee-shirt, postcard or souvenir for the landmark.

TIPS

- Take young children to landmarks that are spectacular and will make a long-lasting impression.
- Think about the time of day you visit. If you want atmosphere, don't go at 'rush hour'.
- Park away from the landmark and walk up to it – for maximum impact!

AGE-RELATED ACTIVITIES

Every child is different; their personalities, interests and talents make them the individuals that we, as parents, try to cater for. The activities suggested in this book for use when visiting or when having visited a location are generic, but there is plenty of scope for making them age-appropriate as well as personal to your own children.

Here is some rough guidance for how to level-up or level-down various learning approaches.

YOUNG CHILDREN (5-7)

- Young children learn best through concrete experiences, i.e. through real-life, touchy-feely, hands-on tasks. Help their learning by giving lots of practical activities.

- A child's brain is constantly growing and forming connections through the stimuli it receives. Enhance this process by offering multi-sensory experiences when you can.

- Concentration spans are short for young children, so keep activities short too. If interest and concentration are dwindling, there won't be much learning, or enjoyment, happening, so make a change.

- Vary the activities that you ask young children to do and mix activities requiring concentration with ones that are more active and less demanding cognitively.

- Help a young learner by 'scaffolding'. What this means is that you help support and structure learning and their understanding of it not for them, but with them. Help with speaking skills by modelling sentence structure or how to construct a question, answer or explanation. With written responses to learning, help them organise the work depending on its genre, e.g. the need for a title, introduction etc.

- It is important to stress that this doesn't mean doing the work for them! Offer advice and help, then step back and let them get on with it themselves. When they are finished, help them check their writing for meaning and also for accuracy.

OLDER CHILDREN (9+)

- Older children should be encouraged to work with more independence and initiative, and less hand-holding. Set them tasks or activities and expect them to get on with them without needing to have you check something every five minutes. Expect them to find things out for themselves, including learning to know where to look, or go to find out information.

- As children get older their ability to learn in abstract ways increases. This means that they are more able to learn from things that are not physical or present in the here and now. For example, a young child will witness an apple falling from a tree as a literal action, whereas an older child will be able to understand and explain the apple falling due to the effect of gravity as a result of a scientific concept.

- This means older children can, and should be, encouraged to make connections between their learning, applying concepts and theories to associated experiences. As and when appropriate, challenge your child to apply their understanding of one thing, like the formation of underground lakes in a cave system, with the acquired understanding of erosion and abrasion when learning about beaches or rivers.

- Children should be expected to be able to concentrate for longer periods as they get older, so encourage them to stick at that sketch they are doing for longer, or to listen attentively during the full tour of a castle. Set the bar high and expect them to achieve.

- Older children grow increasingly able to assimilate and synthesise new learning, i.e. they can listen, read or watch, digest and understand, and then interpret and present their own take on the learning. In other words, they have understood it and can demonstrate that they have. Encourage their ability to do this by asking them to explain things to you, or maybe even explain something in a way that a 5-year-old might understand, or if they were talking to a specialist or expert in the field where precise technical vocabulary would be expected.

SELF-ESTEEM

Self-esteem is one of the most valuable qualities a child can have. Children with a high self-esteem are confident and forthcoming; they are not scared of making mistakes or taking risks (particularly when it comes to new opportunities) and this means they form a growth mindset that ultimately and importantly doesn't hinder their progress and achievement.

Help your child to develop high self-esteem by:
- Listening to them and valuing what they say and do.
- Helping them to realise that not knowing or not being able to do something is not something to be embarrassed about. And there is no such thing as a stupid question!
- Praising the effort, hard work and determination they put into things, not the end product.
- Being patient and understanding and help them to realise that making mistakes is not a bad thing; everybody makes them.

INDEX

DEDICATION

Thank you to our parents for their continued support.

PHOTO AND ILLUSTRATION CREDITS

PHOTOGRAPHS © Tim Meek, with the following exceptions:

Front cover central left photo © David Rose
Page background image texture © Elenamiv/Shutterstock
p4 © Scott J. Carson/Shutterstock | p9 © David White | p12–13 © chbaum/Shutterstock | p15 © jamesdavidphoto/Shutterstock | p17 © TTstudio/Shutterstock | p21 © Alexandra Reinwald/Shutterstock | p25 © Marzolino/Shutterstock | p27 © Awe Inspiring Images/Shutterstock | p29 © maudanros/Shutterstock | p31 © muratart/Shutterstock | p34–35 © astudio/Shutterstock | p36 © littleny/Shutterstock | p39 © Jason Batterham/Shutterstock | p41 © mubus7/Shutterstock | p42 © Chris Warham/Shutterstock | p43 TOP © 1000 Words/Shutterstock | p44 BOTTOM LEFT © j. wootthisak/Shutterstock | p45 TOP © Lesley Rigg/Shutterstock BOTTOM © Featureflash/Shutterstock | p47 © Eugene Sergeev/Shutterstock | p48 BOTTOM LEFT © Keattikorn/Shutterstock BOTTOM RIGHT © Brian S/Shutterstock | p49 © Alfonso Ianniello/Shutterstock | p50 © David Rose | p53 © ShaunWilkinson/Shutterstock | p54 TOP © Carole Castelli/Shutterstock | p56 © 1000 Words/Shutterstock | p57 © Elena Dijour/Shutterstock | p58 © Ron Ellis/Shutterstock | p63 © joingate/Shutterstock | p67 © Steve Lovegrove/Shutterstock | p70 © Mitch Gunn/Shutterstock | p73 © Vogel/Shutterstock | p74 TOP RIGHT © ownza/Shutterstock BOTTOM LEFT © Theas/Shutterstock BOTTOM RIGHT © Anothai Thiansawang/Shutterstock | p75 © Dmitry Kalinovsky/Shutterstock | p76–77 © Ronnie Chua/Shutterstock | p79 © Paul J Martin/Shutterstock | p81 © Michaelpuche/Shutterstock | p84 © DmitriMaruta/Shutterstock | p85 © David Rose | p87 TOP © Sakarin Sawasdinaka/Shutterstock BOTTOM © coxy58/Shutterstock | p89 © 1000 Words/Shutterstock | p92–93 © stocker1970/Shutterstock | p95 © Mike Charles/Shutterstock | p96 © grasslifeisgood/Shutterstock | p99 © Nick Hawkes/Shutterstock | p101 © David Hughes/Shutterstock | p107 © Peter Turner Photography/Shutterstock | p108 TOP RIGHT © bikeriderlondon/Shutterstock BOTTOM LEFT © Philip Bird LRPS CPAGB/Shutterstock | p111 BOTTOM © northallertonman/Shutterstock | p116 BOTTOM LEFT © Bona_natty/Shutterstock BOTTOM RIGHT © Bronwyn Photo/Shutterstock | p119 © Shahid Khan/Shutterstock | p122–123 © Matthew Dixon/Shutterstock | p125 © Ilya D. Gridnev/Shutterstock | p126 TOP © Shebeko/Shutterstock BOTTOM © vladilada/Shutterstock | p127 © Graham Taylor/Shutterstock | p128 BOTTOM LEFT © Amy Johansson/Shutterstock | p129 TOP © kay roxby/Shutterstock | p131 © PHB.cz (Richard Semik)/Shutterstock | p133 © Paolo Bona/Shutterstock | p135 © Michael Stubbs/Shutterstock | p139 © freedomnaruk/Shutterstock | p140 BOTTOM © zebra0209/Shutterstock | p143 © Mark Bridger/Shutterstock | p145 © Stephane Bidouze/Shutterstock | p147 TOP © Thitisan/Shutterstock BOTTOM © Curioso/Shutterstock | p149 © Diana Mower/Shutterstock | p151 © tony mills/Shutterstock | p153 © Steve Pleydell/Shutterstock | p155 © David Hughes/Shutterstock | p156–157 © Bucchi Francesco/Shutterstock | p159 © suriya yapin/Shutterstock | p160 BOTTOM RIGHT © wjarek/Shutterstock | p161 © Savvapanf Photo/Shutterstock | p162 © BOTTOM LEFT Ander Dylan/Shutterstock BOTTOM RIGHT © Jane Rix/Shutterstock | p163 © Ratchapol Yindeesuk/Shutterstock | p165 © T photography/Shutterstock | p167 © Kamira/Shutterstock | p170 © Sara Perez de Arenaza/Shutterstock | p171 © 2630ben/Shutterstock | p172 © Nadiia Gerbish/Shutterstock

ILLUSTRATIONS
Infographic illustrations by Tom Howey On pages 16, 55, 91, 103, 115, 137, 141

Front cover ALL ILLUSTRATIONS © Noka Studio/Shutterstock WITH THE FOLLOWING EXCEPTIONS: WINDMILL, LIGHTHOUSE © kanate/Shutterstock PIE CHART, LIGHTBULB, MAGNIFYING GLASS © Ezhova Marina/Shutterstock
Back cover MAP, TELESCOPE, BOOKS & THOUGHT BUBBLE © Ezhova Marina/Shutterstock ALL OTHER © Noka Studio/Shutterstock
p10 TOP © I can fly/Shutterstock BOTTOM © Ezhova Marina/Shutterstock | p11 BOTH ILLUSTRATIONS © Ezhova Marina/Shutterstock